Church: What, Why, and for Whom?

CHURCH: WHAT, WHY, AND FOR WHOM?

MARK SWEETNAM

WIPF & STOCK · Eugene, Oregon

Wipf and Stock Publishers
199 W 8th Ave, Suite 3
Eugene, OR 97401

Church
What, Why, and for Whom?
By Sweetnam, Mark
Copyright © 2015 by Sweetnam, Mark All rights reserved.
Softcover ISBN-13: 978-1-7252-8926-0
Hardcover ISBN-13: 978-1-7252-8929-1
eBook ISBN-13: 978-1-7252-8927-7
Publication date 10/16/2020
Previously published by Scripture Teaching Library (STL), 2015

This edition is a scanned facsimile of the original edition published in 2015.

CONTENTS

PREFACE

WITH THE EXCEPTION of chapter eleven, the material in this book first appeared in a series of articles in *Believer's Magazine* from February 2014 to January 2015. I am grateful to the editor, John Grant, for the invitation to contribute the series and for his permission to republish it in this form. I am also very grateful to Douglas Mowat for his skilful and sensitive copyediting of the articles. I continue to value the fellowship and encouragement of the brethren with whom I am involved in the work of Scripture Teaching Library, and I am grateful for their comments on the manuscript of this volume. I would also like to thank my father-in-law, Ernest Dover, for his helpful comments on the book as a whole, and especially on Chapter Ten. I deeply appreciate the positive comments of a number of believers who have encouraged me to make the articles available as a single volume. I do so with the prayer that God, in His grace, will be pleased to use this little book for His glory, for the blessing of individual believers, and for the strengthening of assembly testimony.

In writing this book, I have been caused, time and again, to thank God, not just because from a child I was taught the principles of assembly gathering from the Word of God, but because I have been privileged to see those principles practised, quietly and without ostentation, by believers who have given their lives to the assembly, making it, without question, though not without cost, the priority in their lives. Their faithfulness was no mere legalism, nor was it the product of habit. Rather, it was borne of a grasp of the teaching of Scripture, and the clear conviction of the uniqueness, the value, and the importance of 'the house of God, which is the church of the living God, the pillar and ground of the truth' (1 Tim. 3:15). It has been my privilege to meet many such believers, in a variety of places. But as I think about those whose lives have exemplified so much of the truth examined in the chapters that follow, I think especially of my grandparents, for whose interest, influence, and encouragement I will be eternally thankful. '*Beidh cuimhne ar an bhfíréan faoi bheannacht*' (Prov. 10:7).

Mark Sweetnam
DUBLIN, 2015

INTRODUCTION

EIGHT MILES OFF THE SOUTHWEST COAST of Ireland, the Fastnet lighthouse soars 177 feet (54 metres) above the notoriously treacherous Atlantic swell. With a striking beauty that comes from its singularity of presence, the lighthouse seems almost to grow from the jagged slate outcrop known in Irish as *an Carraig Aonair*, the lonely rock. The rock is also known as 'Ireland's Teardrop', earning the name because it was the last bit of Ireland – the final outpost of home – seen by the thousands who, in times of famine and hardship, left Ireland for America.

The Fastnet lighthouse is the second such structure to have stood on this rock. An earlier attempt to provide a lighthouse to warn sailors of the rocks ended in failure beneath the immense destructive power of the battering waves. But this second lighthouse has stood fast amidst the Atlantic waves since it was completed in 1904.

Designed by William Douglass, the Chief Engineer of the Commissioners of Irish Lights, the Fastnet is a remarkable achievement of engineering, constructed from 2,047 dovetailed blocks of Cornish granite, each weighing between 1¾ and 3 tonnes, which were precisely cut to shape in the quarry before being wrapped and transported to Ireland, before being shipped to the rock, where they were carefully fitted together. So careful was the design and so exact the execution that, when the last stone was fitted, the lighthouse was found to have deviated by only six millimetres from the blueprints drawn up seven years earlier. And, in testament to the strength of the foundation and the intelligence of the design, the Fastnet lighthouse has stood for over a century, nightly sweeping its great beam in a five second cycle, carrying out the purpose for which it was built, radiating light in the darkness, providing direction and safety for the traveller.

This is not a book about the Fastnet lighthouse, or any other manmade structure. But it is a book about a far greater structure, which stands on a foundation more impregnable than *an Carraig Aonair*, in an environment more hostile than the Atlantic Ocean, and holding aloft a light brighter and more glorious than that ever marshalled by the Fresnel lens of the Fastnet's great lamp. Like the Fastnet, this structure is an outpost of another land, and like the Fastnet, it has been designed with intelligence and skill in order to discharge its function of beaming forth the light of truth in a world of darkness, turmoil, and danger.

This is a book about the New Testament assembly – the local church. Fundamental to its purpose is the conviction that the local church is a central and vital part of God's purpose in this, the dispensation of grace. And because it is so important, God has given us careful blueprints: the pattern and practice of the local assembly are clearly delineated in the Word of God. Just as the Fastnet lighthouse was designed to bear its light aloft in spite of the inhospitable and hostile conditions in which it is built, so the assembly has been designed in Divine wisdom to be 'the pillar and ground of the truth' (1 Tim. 3:15), to shine the light of testimony in spite of all the opposition that Satan can hurl at it.

So it matters how we meet. The way in which we gather cannot just be the product of culture or convenience, the passage of time or the accretion of tradition. And if we are to follow the blueprint of Scripture with the same accuracy and faithfulness with which the men who built the Fastnet lighthouse followed the plans of William Douglass, we must study it with care.

The aim of this book is to consider some of the most important passages of Scripture relating to the local assembly. It deliberately does not attempt a systematic treatment of the subject. Systematic studies are useful, and a number of excellent treatments of church truth exist. But it is, perhaps, of greater, and certainly of more fundamental, importance to consider the subject biblically – to examine each passage in its contextual setting. In the chapters that follow, in a very elementary way, this is what we seek, with God's help, to do.

A NOTE ON TERMINOLOGY

Throughout this book, the terms 'assembly' and 'church' are both used. As discussed in Chapter One, below, the Greek word translated as 'church' is *ekklesia*, a word which refers to a called-out company of people, and has no reference to a physical building. The origins of the English word 'church' remain the subject of some debate, but it appears first as an architectural term – it described the buildings in which Christians met. William Tyndale, in his translation of the New Testament, avoided using the word 'church' and, instead, used 'congregation' to translate *ekklesia*. If the translators of the *Authorised Version* had followed his example, things would have been a great deal simpler and a good deal clearer. However, their instructions from Richard Bancroft, the conservative Archbishop of Canterbury, explicitly forbade them from lessening the mystique of the established Church by altering any ecclesiastical terms, and so they replaced Tyndale's 'congregation' with the less accurate but more traditional 'church'. In this book, when not quoting from Scripture, the term 'assembly' is generally used as perhaps the most accurate English translation of the Greek *ekklesia*.

CHAPTER ONE

WHAT IS AN ASSEMBLY?

IN MATTHEW 18, the Lord Jesus teaches important lessons about interpersonal relationships. In the opening sections of the chapter He uses the pictures of a child and a sheep to emphasise the vulnerability and the value of, and the consequent seriousness of offending, 'little ones' who believe in Him. As the chapter progresses, the focus shifts from our responsibility not to offend others to our response when they sin against us, a response marked by care to preserve unity and restore fellowship, and a willingness to forgive up to 'seventy times seven' (v. 22). First the erring brother is to be approached individually. If that does not bear fruit, the offended brother, with one or two reliable witnesses, remonstrates further with the offender. If he remains obdurate, a final approach and an ultimate sanction remain: 'And if he shall neglect to hear them, tell it unto the church: but if he neglect to hear the church, let him be unto thee as a heathen man and a publican' (v. 17).

Likely, the disciples would have been rather puzzled by this use of the word 'church'. They knew what it meant: that the word was a compound of two Greek words – ek, or 'out of' and kaleo, meaning 'called' or 'summoned'. They knew of its use to describe political assemblies. They would have known too that the term was used in the Greek translation of the Old Testament to describe the assemblies of the Jewish nation. And they would have remembered the Lord using the word on another occasion when He promised 'I will build My church' (Mt. 16:18). The difficulty for the disciples was not to understand the word, but to comprehend what sort of an *ekklesia* – or assembly – the Lord had in mind.

Their questions were answered as the Lord outlined the characteristics of the Christian *ekklesia*: 'For where two or three are gathered together in My name, there am I in the midst of them' (Mt. 18:20).

Before looking at the detail of this verse, we should note the setting of the Saviour's words. In Matthew 17:22,23 and 20:17–19, the Lord Jesus foretells His sufferings and death. The material between these two passages is structured as chiasmus – a passage arranged in a series of symmetrical parallels around a central, focal point:

    A. 18:8–9
        B. 18:10–14
            C. 18:15–17
                18:18–20
            C. 18:21–35
        B. 19:1–9
    A. 19:10–12

Matthew 18:18–20 is central to this section. The description of the New Testament assembly is placed like a priceless jewel in a carefully crafted setting, emphasising the central importance of the assembly to the teaching of the passage. The context outlines the new relationships and responsibilities that have been brought into being by the death and resurrection of the Lord Jesus. And central to this transformation is the assembly – where these relationships will be manifest.

The lesson is as clear as it is crucial. The assembly is neither an afterthought nor an extra. Rather, it is an essential part of God's purpose for His people in the dispensation of grace. Scripture does not envisage the prospect of maverick believers, living in isolation from others. The 'assembling of ourselves together' (Heb. 10:25) is a vital part of God's plan.

And as we grasp this fact, we do well to ask whether the assembly is central in our lives, or merely something peripheral. If we have never taken our place in assembly fellowship, or if the assembly does not form the focal point of our lives, we do not value it as God does, nor do we understand the unique glory imparted by the presence of Christ.

We should also notice the dispensational context of the church. In this passage, as in Matthew 16, the Lord provides a preview of and a promise for the dispensation of grace. The conditions He describes are unique to the present dispensation. In the dispensation of Law, the Tabernacle and then the Temple were 'the place where [His] honour dwelleth' (Ps. 26:8), the gathering centre for God's people. In the Millennium, too, the 'nations shall come, and say, Come, and let us go up to the mountain of the LORD, and to the house of the God of Jacob' (Micah 4:2). Even during Christ's earthly ministry the conditions outlined in this verse did not exist – the disciples often gathered in His presence, but not in His name. The promise of this verse belongs uniquely to the day of grace.

The unprecedented status that this promise gives to the assembly makes the opening words of Matthew 18:20 most remarkable. As the Lord outlines the composition of the assembly, He makes it clear that fewness of numbers does not equate to the loss of His presence. Even the smallest gathering possible is not too insignificant for His presence. Declining numbers and decreasing strength give us no room for complacency, but they do not prevent us from enjoying the precious promise of the Saviour's presence.

Then the Saviour outlines the *consistency* of the assembly. It is interesting to look at the different ways in which Bible translators have rendered the phrase 'are gathered'. Some use the past tense, others the present. This variety is accounted for by the tense of the verb. It is the perfect participle, and is difficult to render literally in English. 'Having been and being gathered' is close to the sense. The gathering of the assembly

was not something temporary, ad hoc, or occasional. It was a
consistent, constant gathering. In this respect, the assembly
that the Lord Jesus speaks of here differs markedly from the
civil gatherings that the disciples would have been familiar
with. The civil *ekklesia* commenced as people were
summoned together, and ceased to exist as they made their
way to their homes. By contrast, the New Testament assembly
described here has an on-going existence. So, Paul could
write to the 'church of God which is at Corinth' (1 Cor. 1:2),
about the occasions when they came 'together ... into one
place' (1 Cor. 11:20) – the assembly existed even when the
saints were not gathered together. This verb also makes it
clear that this verse is not dealing exclusively with a meeting
for assembly discipline, as outlined in verse 17. That was
clearly an isolated – and exceptional – event, not the enduring
gathering that this verse describes.

Then the Lord outlines the *charter* of the assembly – 'in My
name'. Central to the meaning of 'in My name' is the idea of
authority. In the Old Testament, prophets spoke in the name
of the Lord, claiming His authority for the message they
proclaimed (Deut. 18:19,20; Jer. 14:14,15; 23:25; 27:15). In the
opening days of the dispensation of grace demons would be
cast out in the authority of His name (Mk 16:17). Believers
pray in His name (Jn 14:13,14; 16:23–26). And the assembly
gathered in His name draws its authority from Him. Every
ekklesia had to have an authority for gathering – the
unfortunate town clerk in Ephesus objected to the *ekklesia*
that gathered to oppose the apostles because it was not 'a
lawful assembly' (Acts 19:32, 39, 41). By a lawful assembly, he
meant a gathering vested with the authority of Rome, but the
Saviour outlines for His disciples an infinitely greater
authority. 'His name' was the mandate, as well as the magnet.
It drew them out, and it provided the authority for their
gathering.

A charter outlines authority and imparts privilege; it also
details responsibility. To gather in Christ's name means to
gather in keeping with His character and in obedience to

Divine revelation. We can appreciate the truth of this when we think of prayer. We ask in His name – with His authority. But it would be a strangely insensitive believer who would ask in His name for something that was contrary to His will. So it is with our gathering. We cannot claim to gather in His name, if we are not in submission to His will. The very clause that bestows tremendous privilege imposes a solemn responsibility, a responsibility that should cause us all exercise of heart to ensure that our claim to gather in His name is not an empty assertion but an evident reality.

Finally, the Saviour makes a *commitment* – 'there am I in the midst of them'. Notice His use of the present tense and the personal pronoun. Whenever His people gathered in His name, His presence would be an immediate and intimate reality. It is Matthew alone of the gospel writers who uses the lovely title Emmanuel, 'God with us' (1:23). His gospel closes with the Saviour's promise 'Lo, I am with you alway, even unto the end of the world.' And here, in this great foundational verse of assembly gathering, He promises His presence in the midst of His gathered people.

It would be difficult to imagine a company with a greater status than that described in this passage. The assembly is the company on earth in which Divine administration is manifest and the Divine presence known. May God grant us the insight and appreciation that Jacob received in the chill of a desert night: 'How dreadful is this place! This is none other but the house of God, and this is the gate of heaven' (Gen. 28:17).

CHAPTER TWO

WHAT DOES AN ASSEMBLY DO?

THE DAY OF PENTECOST had been celebrated by the Jews for centuries, but never, in all the centuries of its celebration, had it a greater significance than in the year AD 33. In this year, the feast day was to have an epoch-marking, world-altering importance that reached far beyond the boundaries of the nation. This first Lord's Day marked the beginning of a new dispensation, the fulfilment of Christ's promise (Jn 15:26), and the answer to Christ's prayer (Jn 14:16), as the Holy Spirit was given.

On that day, a new entity came into being. Scripture speaks of it as a building. The Lord Jesus had declared, 'I will build My church' (Mt. 16:18) and it was at Pentecost that that great construction project commenced. The Church is also spoken of as the body of Christ (Eph. 1:23), and as that body came into being it was baptised in the Spirit in a way that was both unprecedented and unrepeatable (1 Cor. 12:13). The Church is also spoken of as the bride of Christ (Rev. 21:9), and, since the moment of her inauguration, her longing has been for the return of the Bridegroom. Since the glorious day of Pentecost, every individual who has trusted the Lord Jesus Christ has been integrated in the building, incorporated in the body, and included in the bride.

The inauguration of the church, the body of Christ, was a unique event. There would only ever be one body of Christ, only ever one bride. But there was another entity that came into existence on the day of Pentecost, which was only the first of many. That entity shared its name and its members with the Church, the body of Christ, but it was neither a microcosm nor a miniature of it. As the gospel spread and as new converts were baptised and gathered together, these churches – or assemblies – were formed throughout the world. Scripture describes them as the 'churches of God' (1 Cor. 11.16; 1 Thess. 2:14; 2 Thess. 1:4) and the 'churches of Christ' (Rom 16:16). The local church in Jerusalem was the first of many, and it set the pattern for countless others down through the centuries.

Thus, Acts 2:41,42 shares a fundamental importance with Matthew 18:20. The latter passage tells us what an assembly is; the former what an assembly does:

> Then they that gladly received his word were baptized: and the same day there were added unto them about three thousand souls. And they continued stedfastly in the apostles' doctrine and fellowship, and in breaking of bread, and in prayers.

Notice that there were prerequisites for being added to the assembly. First of all, salvation was essential. Every one of the three thousand individuals who swelled the ranks of the new church of God had gladly received the Word of God. Peter's message brought them face-to-face with their guilt for rejecting the Messiah, and their complicity in His death. They were 'pricked in their heart' (v. 37). But as they confessed their guilt, Peter unfolded the remarkable – almost incredible – grace of God that was still extended to them. Their belief and salvation gloriously contrast with the commencement of the dispensation of Law, when 'there fell of the people that day about three thousand men' (Exod. 32:28). The assembly in Jerusalem was composed only of those who were saved.

Then those who had been saved were baptised. Baptism was then and is now a prerequisite for assembly fellowship. But, more than this, baptism is a prerequisite for a Christian life. It is not so much that the Bible does not contemplate an unbaptised believer taking his or her place in a local assembly:

Scripture never contemplates the possibility of a believer who does not, at their first opportunity, obey the Lord in baptism. On the day of Pentecost, Jerusalem must have been full of damp and dripping men and women, for all who were saved were baptised before they were added.

Notice that they had to be added. They did not become part of the assembly at conversion, or upon baptism. Being added to the assembly – what Romans 16:2 describes as reception to the assembly – is a distinct step from conversion and baptism. This is one of the crucial differences between the Church which is His body and the local assembly. Salvation places me in the body; it does not automatically make me a member of a local church.

Reception, then, was a separate step, but it was also a significant one. Membership of this assembly was not for dilettantes. The believers in Jerusalem took their position seriously – 'they continued stedfastly'. The word 'stedfastly' has connotations of selfless loyalty, sacrificial devotion, and courageous commitment. These believers were not playing church. Their devotion – practically expressed in the giving of their time, their homes, and their money (vv. 44–46) – might well challenge us, and cause us to re-examine our own 'stedfastness'.

The stedfastness of these believers was expressed in their consistent continuation in the essential activities of an assembly. It is interesting to think about how we might have arranged this list. We might well have given the first place to the breaking of bread. Or, perhaps, we might have put fellowship first. But the Spirit of God puts neither of these at the top of the list. That position is given to 'the apostles' doctrine'. The assembly in Jerusalem was not a gathering of individuals on the basis of a shared social and cultural background. Nor was it merely a gathering of those who had been saved. Rather, it was a company of people bound together by a shared submission to the apostles' teaching and a common obedience to the Word of God.

It was this doctrinal basis that made fellowship real, and gave true significance to its declaration in the breaking of bread. To have fellowship – to 'share in common' – with someone who did not accept the teaching of the apostles would have been impossible, and to break bread with someone not in the fellowship would have been a travesty. Doctrine had to come first.

The saints in Jerusalem on that glorious day did not have a problem with doctrinal disagreement. Sadly, the epistles reveal how short-lived that happy state of affairs was, and two millennia later we see the fruits of error in a baffling array of erroneous doctrine and unscriptural practice. Because they are Christ's, we love believers who do not follow the apostles' doctrine, but we can enjoy only a limited fellowship with them. And, if that agreement and consequent fellowship do not exist, it would be meaningless to break bread together. This being so, salvation and baptism are not sufficient conditions for reception to the local assembly. Obedience – practically, morally, and doctrinally – to the Word of God is essential. And because the assembly is not an open house for all believers regardless of their beliefs and practices, care must be taken in welcoming believers to the fellowship of the assembly. For this reason, we do well to imitate the practice of the assembly at Rome – and of the Apostle Paul – in expecting an unknown believer to bring with him or her a letter of commendation (Rom. 16:1,2).

So we can learn much from the order of this list. But, as we do so, let us not miss the sweetness and simplicity of the practices outlined here. The assembly at Jerusalem enjoyed Divine communication, as God spoke through His Word, and as believers spoke to God in prayer. It enjoyed unity, and fellowship. Many of these believers had been rejected by their families; they were opposed by their nation. But they had gained far more than they had lost – not just eternal life, but fellowship with other believers, expressed week-by-week, as they obeyed the command of their Lord. Nor was their unity limited to an hour-and-a-half on a Lord's Day morning. The unity of the believers was so real, so deep, that they 'had all things common' (v. 44). The balance of New Testament revelation makes it clear that this sharing of possessions was an exceptional feature, but the unity it expressed was not, and should not be.

The world of the twenty-first century is immeasurably different from that of the first century. If Peter and Paul were to find themselves in a modern city they would soon learn that it was a strange and confusing place. But amidst the fumes and the noise, the advertising, and the gadgets, would they still find, by the grace of God, and in testament to the durability of the Divine pattern, companies of those who continue stedfastly in the apostles' doctrine, and fellowship, and in breaking of bread, and prayers? May we resemble that first assembly in Jerusalem, in the Person to Whom we gather, the pattern we follow, and our passion for the local assembly where Christ meets with His own.

CHAPTER THREE

WHAT (AND WHOM) IS AN ASSEMBLY FOR?

THERE ARE TWO QUESTIONS that are central to creating, understanding, or evaluating any design. The first is, 'Whom is it for?'; the second, 'What purpose does it serve?' If we fail to ask, and correctly answer, these questions, our understanding of the design we are considering will remain deeply deficient.

This is as true in spiritual things as in secular, and it is certainly the case when we consider the local assembly. Unless we grasp the truth of whom and what the assembly is for, we risk succumbing to serious, and sadly common, misunderstandings about the nature of the church of God.

It is worth remembering that the assembly does have a design, and that that design is laid down in Scripture. God has not left His people in any doubt as to where and how they should gather. We do not need to rely on the opinions of men or the expectations of society. Assembly practice is not the product of gradual development, an accretion of customs drawn from different cultures and times. Rather, God's Word provides the pattern, the design, for the collective testimony of His people. Paul emphasised this as he wrote to the believers in Corinth:

> According to the grace of God which is given unto me, as a wise masterbuilder, I have laid the foundation, and another buildeth thereon. But let every man take heed

how he buildeth thereupon. For other foundation can
no man lay than that is laid, which is Jesus Christ (1
Cor. 3:10,11).

The metaphor of building indicates not just activity but
accuracy. The plans have been drawn, the foundation laid,
and we must, therefore, take heed as we build. And though
we often consider the teaching of this passage as to what we
build, notice that the apostle speaks of how we build, for
unless we follow the blueprints, our contribution will be of
little value.

The local assembly, then, is not – and should not be – a
haphazard accident. It must be the implementation of Divine
design, an entity that accords with the pattern of Scripture.
And this being so, we can – and should – ask, 'Whom is the
assembly for?' For some the answer is, 'For the world'. They
emphasise the responsibility of believers to preach the gospel,
and encourage churches to be 'seeker-friendly', to be relevant
to contemporary society, and to eliminate anything that
might be off-putting to the unsaved, even if this means
ignoring the Word of God. The covered heads and silence of
the sisters, the dignity and decorum of worship, the
unadorned simplicity of Scriptural preaching are, all too
often, deemed unattractive, and so must be jettisoned lest our
outreach be compromised. There is, of course, no doubt that
we have a clear responsibility to preach the gospel. We should
welcome unbelievers to our gatherings, and they should be
impressed with the evidence of the Divine presence amongst
us (1 Cor. 14:23–25). We must 'shine as lights in the world;
Holding forth the word of life' (Phil. 2:15,16). But we cannot
disregard the teaching of Scripture just to be relevant to the
world, for the assembly is not for society.

Others will answer the question by asserting that the
assembly is for the believers who gather there. It is 'our
assembly', even 'my assembly', and its priority must be the
convenience and comfort of those who gather. It must not
make unreasonable demands on our time, our resources, or

our minds. It must be a cosy place where we are stimulated and entertained, where no great demands are made upon us. Again, there is no doubt that the assembly should be a place where the saints are at home, where we are fed, and where our spiritual wellbeing is increased. But we cannot make our comfort the guiding principle of our gatherings, for the assembly is not primarily for the saints.

For whom, then, is the assembly designed? 1 Timothy 3:15 gives us the answer – it is 'the house of God, which is the church of the living God'. The assembly is God's – it belongs to Him, and is for Him. Paul emphasised the same fact to the Corinthian believers: 'ye are God's husbandry, ye are God's building (1 Cor. 3:9). And, in his charge to the Ephesian elders he emphasised not just God's ownership of the assembly in Ephesus, but the price of that ownership: 'feed the church of God, which He hath purchased with His own blood' (Acts 20:28).

It would be difficult to overstate the importance of this truth. If the assembly is for God, what matters is not whether our practice is attractive to the world or appealing to the saints, but whether it is acceptable to Him. If the assembly is for God, my service there must not simply be sufficient to impress my brethren or please the overseers, but suitable to be offered as worship to Him. And if the assembly is God's and is for God, it deserves every ounce of commitment, of ability, of effort that I can muster.

The context of 1 Timothy 3:15 demonstrates this importance. The careful directions for church order given in this chapter – and in the epistle as a whole – matter, because the assembly is God's. It is His house, a term that speaks of His ownership, but also of His authority. I have no right to redecorate my neighbour's house, or to rearrange his furniture. How then could I ever think I had the right to alter the arrangements that the living God has made for His house? They matter too because of the vitally important purpose that the assembly has. The 'house of God, which is the church of the living God' is, Paul tells us, 'the pillar and ground

['bulwark', NET] of the truth'. The assembly has a two-fold
function in relation to truth. It preserves it and protects it;
displays it and defends it; holds it forth, and holds it fast. And
while 'the truth' includes all that God has revealed, Paul goes
on to outline some of the most profound elements of the
truth that the assembly maintains: 'And without controversy
great is the mystery of godliness: God was manifest in the
flesh, justified in the Spirit, seen of angels, preached unto the
Gentiles, believed on in the world, received up into glory'.
The assembly has the responsibility to preach the gospel, to
teach the essentials of Christian conduct, and the principles
of assembly gathering. But its responsibility goes far beyond
this. The truth of Who Christ is, and of what He has done
have been entrusted to us to be preserved and
communicated.

In his first epistle to Timothy Paul tells us how the assembly
functions as 'the pillar and ground of the truth' (3.15), and in
his second epistle, 'the things that thou hast heard of me
among many witnesses, the same commit thou to faithful
men, who shall be able to teach others also' (2:2). Truth is
passed from generation to generation, entrusted to 'faithful
men' 'among many witnesses', accredited as the authentic
truth of God, precious and powerful in every age.

And it is in the assembly that this is to happen. In the first
chapter of the second epistle the family is the place of teaching,
where Timothy received his grounding in the Scriptures from a
faithful grandmother and mother. The value of that instruction
was incalculable, and many of us have cause to thank God for
godly mothers and grandmothers who grounded us in the Word
of God. Besides the family, the only institution that Paul
envisages for the transmission of truth is the assembly. No
human institution or expedient, no subsection of, or
supplement to, the assembly can be described as 'the pillar and
ground of the truth'. That function is uniquely reserved for the
local assembly, where all the truth of God's Word can be
publicly and accountably communicated to all of God's people

by spiritually gifted brethren who are 'apt to teach' (1 Tim. 3:2; 2 Tim. 2.24).

The assembly's purpose is a lofty one. To be the repository of Divine truth is both a unique privilege and a heavy responsibility. And this purpose will not be achieved automatically. Exercise and effort will be required on the part of those who have the responsibility of oversight and those who have been gifted to teach. Our ministry will need to grow in depth and breadth, for all the 'counsel of God' (Acts 20:27) must be communicated. This exercise will result, and this effort seem light, if we are gripped by the conviction that our primary responsibility as an assembly of the Lord's people is to do His will and proclaim His Word. A clear understanding of the purpose of the assembly should cause us to examine our approach, to re-evaluate our activity, to ensure that our solemn duty is discharged. May we, collectively, as well as individually, be ever, only, all for Him.

CHAPTER FOUR

THE LORD'S SUPPER (1)

IT WAS DARK IN JERUSALEM. Here and there the chill gloom of the April night was broken by the cheerful warmth of the watchmen's braziers. But their flickering flames were powerless to dispel the blackness of the devilish plot whose dark coils moved in the city streets. Even in the warmth and brightness of the upper room, the shadows gathered. Pride and ambition had raised their loathsome heads, and the disciples had been disturbed and dismayed by talk of betrayal. But then the betrayer went out into the darkness of the night, to complete his fateful transaction and lead the malevolent mob to the Saviour's wonted place of prayer. In the minutes after his departure the Lord Jesus did something irreducibly simple and inexhaustibly profound:

> And as they were eating, Jesus took bread, and blessed it, and brake it, and gave it to the disciples, and said, 'Take, eat; this is My body'. And He took the cup, and gave thanks, and gave it to them, saying, 'Drink ye all of it; For this is My blood of the new testament, which is shed for many, for the remission of sins' (Mt. 26:26–28).

Each of the synoptic gospels records the institution of the Lord's Supper and, in 1 Corinthians 11, Paul recounts the direct revelation that he received. The book of Acts records its observance by local assemblies (Acts 2:42). Though it was not instituted on the first day of the week, the example of the assembly at Troas demonstrates that it quickly became specially identified with the Lord's Day (Acts 20:7).

There is a very precious simplicity about the
remembrance that the Saviour instituted. It required no
complex apparatus. Only bread and wine were necessary to
obey the Lord's command. And this simplicity has made it
possible for His command to be obeyed all over the world.
In homes and halls, in caves and under hedges, beneath the
burning sun and amidst freezing blizzards, in diverse
cultures and climates, Christ's disciples have been able, in
Scriptural simplicity, to remember Him. This simplicity
must be safeguarded and we must be ever watchful to
identify and oppose any attempt to add to the Scriptural
pattern, to introduce human laws or expedients. C.F. Hogg's
warning is stark, but not overstated: 'To make any particular
person, or an act not prescribed in Scripture essential to the
right observance of the ordinance, is to move on a way that
lies through ritualism to clerisy and priestcraft'.* Through
the centuries, men have sought to improve upon what the
Saviour instituted. They have added rituals and rules in the
name of enhancing the solemnity or emphasising the
sacredness of the supper. And yet, there can be nothing so
sacred, so solemn, and yet so gloriously joyful as
remembering the Lord in scriptural simplicity, by breaking
bread, and drinking wine.

For all this simplicity, there is, nonetheless, a profound
significance to the Lord's Supper. As we keep it we are
obeying a command, remembering a Person, announcing a
death, and anticipating a hope.

We are commanded to eat the Lord's Supper. When the
Saviour said, 'this do' (Lk. 22:19), He was not making a
request or a suggestion, but issuing a command. It is His
intention, as well as His desire, that His disciples faithfully
continue to break bread in remembrance of Him, until His
return. The Lord's Supper is not an optional extra, but a
vital part of the Christian life, as God would have us live it.
If there were no other reason to break bread, no other

---

* *What Saith the Scripture?* (London, 1947), p. 160.

blessing associated with it, the bare fact that Christ commanded it should be sufficient to ensure that we are never lightly absent from the gathering. And, while sickness and family responsibilities will at times curtail our ability to do as He commanded, we should order our lives so as to minimise the occasions when we are absent from the Supper. This priority may have its implications for my employment. It will certainly impose limits upon when and where I spend my holidays. But such sacrifices are surely hardly to be weighed against the privilege of remembering our Saviour, and showing the Lord's death, until He comes again. We will not lose by our obedient attendance at the Lord's Supper, but, like Thomas in John 20, we will find that our absence makes us the poorer, for it results in the loss of time spent with the Saviour, learning more of His Person and His ways.

As we eat the Lord's Supper, we obey His command. We must appreciate, however, that merely taking and consuming the emblems only fulfils part of the Lord's command – we must remember Him. Knowing well how fickle our minds can be, the Lord instituted the Supper as a prophylactic against forgetfulness. As we gather, we call Him to mind. Our hearts swell with thoughts of all that He is, of all that He became, of all that He has done and will do. Just as Joseph's brothers told his father 'of all [his] glory in Egypt' (Gen. 45:13), we delight to tell the Father of the glories of His resplendent Son. We do so with thanksgiving and gladness (Mt. 26:26; Mk 14:22; 1 Cor. 11:24). Scripture never speaks of the Breaking of Bread as a worship meeting – worship should have far too great a role in our lives to permit of its being confined to one hour in the week. Nonetheless, we cannot remember Him without worshipping. And as we worship our thoughts should be filled with Him. On this occasion it is inappropriate to speak of our blessings, our emotions, or our responsibilities, for we are remembering Him, and praise and not prayer must result as our focus rests wholly on His glorious Person.

But remembering Him is only part of what we do. As we break bread we proclaim His death: 'For as often as ye eat this bread, and drink this cup, ye do shew ['announce', JND, 'proclaim', NET] the Lord's death till He come' (1 Cor. 11.26). The emblems themselves show His death, for it is only in death that body and blood are separated. But the word 'shew' always refers to speech, and to public proclamation. On ten of the seventeen occasions that it is used in the New Testament it is translated as 'preach'. As we gather to 'remember Him' we can range eternity; but as we proclaim His death our focus narrows to the day, and to the hours in which He gave Himself to the abuse of men and the sufferings of the cross. And if we are to proclaim His death, we must meditate upon it, as it is revealed in Scripture. What an occupation this is, to listen to the deepest cries of the Saviour's soul as anticipated in prophecy, to watch His agony in the gospel records, and to appreciate its implications as unfolded in the epistles. And how blest, in the midst of a dark and dying world, to proclaim His death as we break the bread and drink from the cup.

And we do it 'till He come'. Our worship must bring us to Calvary, but it cannot leave us there, for we gather around a risen Christ. Even as we proclaim the Saviour's passion, we rejoice in His triumph, and anticipate a glorious prospect. The broken bread and outpoured wine, in all their beautiful symbolism are only temporary, 'sweet memorials till the Lord call us round His heavenly board'. When the day breaks, 'the shadows flee away' (Song 4:6), and, possessing the reality, we will no longer need the symbols. One day we will break bread for the last time. May we value each opportunity that remains to obey our Lord in remembering His Person, proclaiming His passion, and anticipating with renewed ardour the glorious prospect of His return.

Sweet feast of love Divine!
'Tis grace that makes us free
To feed upon this bread and wine

In memory, Lord, of Thee.
But if this glimpse of love
Is so Divinely sweet,
What will it be, O Lord, above,
Thy gladdening smile to meet?
(Edward Denny)

CHAPTER FIVE

THE LORD'S SUPPER (2)

IN THE UPPER ROOM, the same night in which He was being betrayed, the Lord Jesus took bread and a cup of wine and instituted the Lord's Supper. The remembrance that He ordained for His own was marked by a sweet simplicity, and a profound significance. The act of eating and drinking come freighted with symbolism that contributes to the meaning of the Lord's Supper.

Throughout history, and in all cultures, sharing a meal is an important symbol of fellowship, and the Lord's Supper is no exception. Observing it requires physical togetherness – the disciples in Troas 'came together to break bread' (Acts 20:7), and the believers at Corinth came 'together ... into one place' (1 Cor. 11:20).

But, as Paul explains in 1 Corinthians 10, the breaking of bread demonstrates a unity and proclaims a fellowship that goes beyond mere physical co-location. It proclaims our fellowship with Christ: 'The cup of blessing which we bless, is it not the communion of the blood of Christ? The bread which we break, is it not the communion of the body of Christ?' (v. 16). To understand this verse we need to notice the two comparisons that Paul draws. First, he points out, under the Jewish order, fleshly sacrifices were offered upon a literal altar, and as the offerer took and ate his portion of the peace offering, he partook of the altar (v. 18). He did not literally bite a chunk from the altar of burnt offering, but, by eating his portion of the peace offering he expressed his fellowship with the altar and his part in the sacrifice. Similarly, those who sat at meat in the idol's temple were doing more than eating a meal. The act of eating from 'the table of demons' and drinking from 'the cup of demons' (v. 21, JND) was an expression of fellowship with the demons who were connected with the idol. The 'communion of' the body and blood of Christ (also translated as 'a participation in' (ESV) and 'the sharing of' (NET)) must be understood in the same way. As we partake of the elements we demonstrate our oneness with Christ, our part in His sacrifice, and in the blessings that have flowed from that sacrifice.

In the breaking of bread, then, we declare fellowship with Christ, vertically. But we also bear witness to a horizontal fellowship, declaring our unity with those who partake. When we gather together to bless the cup, as we add our 'Amen' to the words of the brother who audibly gives thanks, and to break the bread, as we take our portion from the loaf, we proclaim that 'we being many are one bread, and one body: for we are all partakers of that one bread' (1 Cor. 10:17). In the context, it is not the unity of all believers that is expressed but the unity of those who partake. It is true that Paul most often uses the metaphor of the body to refer to the dispensational Church that includes all believers of this Church age. It is important to notice, however, that verse 16 sets the parameters for our understanding of verse 17. And verse 16 clearly describes the action of a gathered company – breaking 'the bread' and blessing 'the cup'. Apart, perhaps, from a very short period in the immediate aftermath of Pentecost when all who were believers were gathered in assembly fellowship at Jerusalem, the Church, the body of Christ, could never have been said to have given thanks for the cup, or broken the bread. And there is nothing to indicate any change in the meaning of 'we' between the verses. We bless, we break, and 'because there is one bread, we who are many are one body, for we all share the one bread' (v. 17, NET). It would be difficult to think of a more eloquent expression of unity than that which the Lord has given. At the commencement of the breaking of bread, the one loaf sits as one unified object. At the end of the meeting it has been divided into many pieces, and each piece has become part of a believer. And so we proclaim not just our unity with Christ, but also the bond that unites us one to the other.

The unity we affirm as we break bread has two vital implications. The first implication is Paul's main point in this section of the epistle. If we express fellowship with Christ and our fellow-believers, we must ensure that we are free from other contradictory or contaminating fellowships. 'Ye cannot drink the cup of the Lord, and the cup of devils: ye cannot be partakers of the Lord's table, and of the table of devils' (1 Cor. 10:21). The man who sits at the Lord's Table on Sunday morning should not be found at a meal in an idol's temple throughout the week. While the expression 'the Lord's Table' has often been understood as a description of believers' continual enjoyment of God's provision, such an interpretation places considerable strain upon the language of this passage. Not only does the word 'partaking' in this verse indicate a physical – rather than a spiritual – participation, Paul's words require us to understand partaking of the Lord's Table as a distinct, discrete, and visible event, comparable to the act of sitting at the idol feast. Thus, a proper understanding of the Lord's Supper has important ethical implications – it will keep us pure in a defiling world. The second implication of the fellowship we express as we break bread is also vital: the fellowship we profess must exist practically.

Second, the breaking of bread has an individual, as well as a communal, aspect. Eating and drinking are personal acts. I cannot delegate someone else to eat for me, or to drink on my behalf. It is something I must do for myself. Each of the Lord's commands – 'take', 'eat', 'drink' – require a personal obedience from each individual. It is not sufficient to be present while He is remembered, or to listen to others remember Him. We must each remember – audibly or inaudibly. And surely this should not seem an onerous duty, but the inevitable result of our occupation with Himself. Strange and sad it is if so great a subject should lose its wonder, if we are reduced to uttering the same conglomeration of quotations and clichés week by week. May God grant us an ever fresh and ever deepening appreciation of His Son, and may we resolve: 'Yea, while a breath, a pulse remains, I will remember Thee'.*

And the individual nature of the act also has important and serious implications. Paul stresses the responsibility of each believer:

> let a man examine himself, and so let him eat of that bread, and drink of that cup. For he that eateth and drinketh unworthily, eateth and drinketh damnation to himself, not discerning the Lord's body (1 Cor. 11:28,29).

The Corinthian believers had begun to treat the Lord's Supper as though it were just another meal, and their lack of care had dire personal consequences. Many were 'weak and sickly', and some had even died. Their example stands as a stark warning to us.

Third, eating and drinking are inextricably linked with nourishment. In our everyday lives, it is by eating and drinking that our physical life is maintained, and our physical strength increased. God's Word teaches neither trans- nor con-substantiation. As we observe the Lord's Supper, the loaf and the cup neither become nor contain the body and blood of the Lord Jesus. They remain, at all times, 'Only bread and only wine'. Yet we could hardly sit down to remember the Lord Jesus and to obey His command, and not find our souls nourished, and 'our feeble love...fed'. The Lord's Supper was instituted by Christ for our blessing, and it deepens our appreciation of and fellowship with Christ and strengthens our souls to meet the demands of another week. Bread and wine are first mentioned in Scripture in Genesis 14:18, when Melchizedek met Abraham, and strengthened him for his

---

* James Montgomery, 'According to Thy gracious word', *Believer's Hymn Book*, no. 5.

encounter with the king of Sodom. Week-by-week, and day-by-day, we face a more formidable foe, and nothing will fortify us for that encounter like our remembrance of our Saviour, His sacrifice, and His return.

On the first day of each week we break bread, giving the act the preeminent place in our lives. Our partaking may last only seconds, the emblems circulate in only minutes, and the whole meeting last less than a couple of hours. But that simple act has implications and effects that infiltrate our whole week, and every aspect of our lives. Let us remember that we come to the Lord's Table, to partake of the Lord's Supper. The Supper is stamped with His character and His authority, and the apprehension of what we do as we sit down with Him should loom large in our lives, dominating our thoughts and directing our deeds on every day of the week.

CHAPTER SIX

HEADSHIP IN THE ASSEMBLY

AT MOUNT SINAI God outlined a detailed set of instructions for Israel's worship. As befitted an earthly people, Jewish priests served God in a physical sanctuary, offering physical sacrifices on a physical altar. Sounds, smells, and sights all played an important role in their religious life. That dispensation and that system of worship have alike come to an end. Now, the Father is to be worshipped without geographical or ethnic distinctions, 'in spirit and in truth' (Jn 4:23). In this dispensation believers serve as spiritual priests, offering spiritual sacrifices in a spiritual sanctuary.

Notwithstanding this, the Holy Spirit has given three ordinances for the Church age that give physical expression to spiritual realities. The truth attested by each of these ordinances is intimately related to the Person and work of our Lord Jesus Christ, and our relationship with Him. In baptism, the physical act eloquently attests that the believer has died with Christ, and has been raised again with Him. Similarly, in the Lord's Supper, the physical act of breaking the bread and drinking from the cup proclaims the Lord's death, and our fellowship with Him.

The third of these ordinances is described in 1 Corinthians 11:1–16. In this passage we learn that the uncovered heads of men and the covered heads of women in the gatherings of the assembly are physical signs that give expression to vital scriptural – and Christological – truth.

Few passages of God's Word have produced such controversy as these verses. The reason for this does not lie in Scripture. While there are some difficult verses in the passage, the implications of its teaching are very clear. The difficulty lies with society. The teaching of this passage cuts across the beliefs and practices of this feminist age. All too often, in the clash between Scripture and society, it is the strident cry of society that is heard and heeded, and the clear commands of God's Word set aside. If it were not for the fundamental seriousness of seeing Scripture denigrated and disregarded, there would be something risible in the hermeneutical contortions and exegetical gymnastics performed by expositors who will not allow God's Word to mean what it says and refuse to yield to the plain – though unpopular – teaching of these verses.

We must approach this passage, then, in a spirit of submissiveness, prepared to understand and obey. And, as we consider it, we should notice the practical implications, the spiritual import, and the importance of these verses.

In considering the implications of this ordinance, note the context to which it applies. The passage forms part of a section of the epistle that is dealing especially with the gatherings of a local assembly, and is bookended by sections that deal unambiguously with the meetings of the assembly (1 Cor. 11:17). Furthermore, verse 16 sets the ordinance in the context of the 'church of God'. The assembly setting is in view. Scripture does not proscribe the use of the head covering in other contexts, but prescribes it only for the gatherings of the local assembly. In other contexts, our practice should be guided by spiritual intelligence, common sense, and good manners. When there is legitimate room for uncertainty – in our own mind, or the minds of others – it is best to err on the side of caution.

Note the clarity of the instructions. There really is no room for confusion as to the practical effects of the two sets of instructions in the passage. First, the main point of this passage is that, in the assembly, men's heads should be uncovered, and women's heads covered. It is regrettable that the translators of the ESV, amongst others, have confused matters by translating 'man' as 'husband' in verse 3 and 'woman' as 'wife' in verses 3, 5, 6, and 13. That this decision is entirely without contextual justification is demonstrated by the fact that the same words are also translated as 'man' and 'woman' in this passage. Paul's appeal to creatorial order makes it clear that men and women are in view throughout, not just husbands and wives.

Second, while the subject of head covering is Paul's main concern in these verses, his discussion of the importance of maintaining creatorial order, and the distinction between the sexes, leads to another pair of instructions. Men should not wear their hair long, for 'Doth not even nature itself teach you, that, if a man have long hair, it is a shame unto him?' (v. 14). By the same token, it 'is a glory' (v. 15) for a woman to have long hair, but it is 'a shame for a woman to be shorn or shaven' (v. 6).

These are practical instructions. To obey them may bring us into conflict with the fluctuating fashions of the world, and there is real reproach and real cost associated with obedience. But 'We ought to obey God rather than men' (Acts 5:29), assured that the cost of that obedience is assessed and appreciated by our Lord.

Obedience to the Word of God is its own motive. But our obedience to this ordinance should not be blind, for its spiritual import is clearly outlined. Notice that Paul deals with two pairs of symbols. The long hair of the woman and the short hair of the man proclaim a creatorial distinction. When God made Eve, He was not just making another Adam in different packaging. Rather, Eve was 'a help meet for' Adam, 'a companion for him who corresponds to him' (Gen. 2:18, NET). The woman was created 'for the man' (1 Cor. 11:9), to be his complement, with strengths that would answer his weaknesses, and weaknesses matched by his strengths. In a world where differentiation between the sexes is denied,

Christian men and women should give testimony, by their appearance, to Divine order and design.

As the assembly gathers, the temporary covering of the women's heads and the temporary uncovering of the men's gives testimony to Christological, as well as to creatorial, truth. This symbol demonstrates the headship of Christ in the assembly. 'The head of the woman is the man' (v. 3), and she covers her physical head as a symbol that, in the assembly, man's glory is to be hidden. 'The head of every man is Christ' (v. 3), and the man uncovers his physical head as a symbol that it is Christ's glory that is seen in the assembly, and Christ's authority that is owned. Thus a simple symbol has a profound significance, and our submission to the teaching of this passage allows us to glorify our Lord, and give Him His rightful place.

This helps us to grasp the importance of the symbol, and Paul underscores this throughout the passage. Firstly, he stresses the origins of the message. The teaching of this passage is part of the ordinances (or traditions) that he delivered to the Corinthian believers (v. 2). Paul uses the word 'delivered' in this way on two other occasions in the epistle – in 1 Corinthians 11:23 about the order of the Lord's Supper and in 1 Corinthians 15:3 of the gospel. On each of these occasions he is speaking of the passing on of Divinely revealed truth. Thus, we cannot simply dismiss this passage as reflecting Paul's personal preferences. This teaching originated in the ineffable wisdom of the eternal God.

Head covering is important, too, because of the observers. Paul reminds the Corinthians that their gatherings are observed by angels: 'For this reason a woman should have a symbol of authority on her head, because of the angels' (v. 10, NET). Angels know better than most the fearful consequences that flow from the denial of Divine headship. They witnessed those consequences in the rebellion of Satan, and again in the fall of Adam. They have seen, too, perfect submission to Divine headship in the life of the Lord Jesus. Now they look on as we gather, and they must surely wonder as something of the submission of Christ is seen in the redeemed sons of Adam's race.

Paul's teaching is important because of the practice of others. He makes it clear that this ordinance is not a personal notion or a practice peculiar to Corinth. 'But if any man seem to be contentious, we have no such custom, neither the churches of God' (v. 16). Dissension from, or disobedience to, this teaching was unknown to the apostles ('we' of the verse), or amongst the churches of God. How blessed it must have been to see every assembly united by their obedience to God's Word, proclaiming the headship of Christ, regardless of the contradictory expectations of society, and how blessed it would be in our day to see believers similarly united, walking by the same rule, and minding the same thing (Phil. 3:16).

CHAPTER SEVEN

GIFT IN THE ASSEMBLY

IN THE LONG HISTORY of human construction, one edifice stands out as distinct. It was not the biggest – its dimensions were modest. It was not the most durable – it was only a tent. But for all that, the Tabernacle was one of the most remarkable structures that the world has seen. The secret of its unique importance lay in its purpose – it was the 'house of God' (1 Chron. 6:48 etc.), where Jehovah dwelt, the 'tent of meeting' (Exod. 27:21 etc., JND), where God's people could approach Him, the 'tent of witness' (Acts 7:44, ESV), that stood as a testimony to the character of God, and embodied so many precious lessons about the Lord Jesus Christ.

Its purpose gives the Tabernacle a unique distinction, but its construction, too, was remarkable. It called for the highest skills of tentmakers and tailors, of embroiderers and goldsmiths, of carpenters and carvers. To attempt an accurate reconstruction would be a difficult and costly business. It is striking, therefore, that the original was erected by a band of travelling refugees. They had received harsh instruction in brick making and building under the lash of the taskmaster's whip. But the Tabernacle, for all of the variety of its design, contained not a single brick. Their inexperience posed no difficulty for God. He selected Bezaleel, and 'filled him with the Spirit of God, in wisdom, in understanding, and in knowledge, and in all manner of workmanship' (Exod. 35:31). Along with Aholiab, Bezaleel was Divinely equipped to do what he could never have achieved on the basis of his own education or experience. It was spiritual ability and spiritual exercise that mattered when building the house of God.

What was true of the Tabernacle is true of the house of God in this dispensation. God, who provided with such singular care for the fittings of His earthly house, does not rely on natural talent or training for the building and beautification of the assembly. Rather, He equips individuals for His service, giving them gifts that enable them to fulfil roles and shoulder responsibilities for which their own abilities would be inadequate. Three passages in the New Testament contain crucial lessons about the distribution and operation of spiritual gifts: Romans 12:1–21; 1 Corinthians 12:1–31 and Ephesians 4:1–19. An exhaustive treatment is beyond the scope of this chapter, but there are a number of important lessons that we should note.

It is useful to begin by thinking about the name given to these spiritual abilities. They are called 'gifts', a word that translates the Greek word *charisma*, which is closely linked with *charis*, or 'grace'. This term has been hijacked by the so-called charismatic movement, and is often used to describe just the spectacular sign gifts, which have now been brought to an end (1 Cor. 13:8–10). But, in its scriptural usage, the word applies to every gift of God. The enabling gifts of the Spirit are gifts of grace – they are not earned or deserved, have nothing to do with the merits of the recipient, and they afford no room for boasting.

The word 'gift' also points to the Giver of the gift. In Romans 12, the gifts are seen as given by God the Father (v. 3), in 1 Corinthians 12 by the Holy Spirit (v. 7), and in Ephesians 4 by the risen Christ (vv. 8–10). In the first two passages, gifts are given to individuals. In Ephesians, where the Church in its dispensational aspect is in view, gifted individuals are seen as gifts to the Church, just as God gave 'the Levites as a gift to Aaron and to his sons from among the children of Israel' (Num. 8:19). Spiritual abilities, and the individuals who possess them, are the gift of the Godhead to meet the need of the Church the Body of Christ and to meet the need of local assemblies. That is the goal of these gifts – 'for the perfecting of the saints, for the work of the ministry, for the edifying of the body of Christ' (Eph. 4:12).

These gifts are universal. That is, there is no believer – male or female, old or young, educated or untutored – who has not been entrusted with a spiritual gift. 'The manifestation of the Spirit is given to every man to profit withal' (1 Cor. 12:7; see also 1 Pet. 4:10). In these passages, the translation disguises what the text makes clear: the word 'man' does not occur in the original. Each believer, then, has been given a gift, a 'manifestation of the Spirit', which they are to use for the profit and blessing of all.

So, even as Paul tells us that gift is universal, he also makes it clear that gift is something very individual – there are, he points out, 'diversities of gifts' (1 Cor. 12:4). And, just as no one is to glory in their gift, so no one is to despise it, or covet another's, for each gift is as necessary to the healthy and happy functioning of the assembly as is the differentiated but interdependent operation of the parts of the body. I will make my most valuable contribution to the assembly, not when I am trying to emulate the gift of others, or attempting a task for which I have not been fitted, but when I humbly, diligently, and dependently exercise the gift that God, in grace, has given me.

It is vital to understand that diligence is needed in the exercise and development of gift. The fact that we rely utterly upon Divine enablement by the power of the Holy Spirit does not relieve us of the responsibility to exert ourselves in the exercise of our gift. Paul reminded Timothy of this, urging him first of all not to neglect his gift (1 Tim. 4:14), and later, to 'stir up the gift of God, which is in thee' (2 Tim. 1:6). These exhortations have no less force for us. It is all too possible for a God-given gift to be neglected, left to wither and waste rather than being used for the glory of God and the blessing of His people. May God preserve us from the tragedy of undeveloped gift! Rather, let us obey in our own lives the injunction of the apostle, and 'stir up' our gift. 'Stir up' literally means 'to fan into flame' and conveys not just the effort and exertion that is involved, but also the potential and power of a gift ablaze for God's use.

Gift, then, brings with it a burden of responsibility. Like the servants who traded with their master's talents (Mt. 25:14–30), we will be held accountable for our use of the resources that God has given to us. But if individual believers are responsible to exercise and develop their gift, assemblies – and overseers – are also responsible to identify and encourage, and give opportunity to gift. In Exodus 31, God told Moses that He had equipped Bezaleel to oversee the fitting out of the Tabernacle. But it is only in Exodus 35 that Moses publicly recognises Bezaleel's gift, giving him the opportunity to employ it. And that opportunity mattered. Not just because Bezaleel got to use his gift – that was only a secondary consideration – but because Bezaleel's faithful exercise of his gift was vital for the building and beautification of the house of God.

We would like to think that gift would invariably be recognised and encouraged, but, sadly, this is not always the case. Even Timothy did not always receive the encouragement of the assemblies amongst which he ministered. Paul had to exhort the Corinthians to 'see that he may be with you without fear' and warned them not to 'despise' the young man as he carried on 'the work of the Lord' (1 Cor. 16:10,11). Corinth was in a poor state, but they were not the last assembly to run the risk of stifling gift by intimidating and discouraging a gifted servant of God. How much better to follow the example of Aquila and Priscilla, whose spiritual and tactful interest in Apollos played a vital role in enhancing his usefulness for God.

God still provides gifts to meet the needs of each local assembly. If there seems to be a lack of gift in our assembly, if we find ourselves to be always relying on the gift of brethren from elsewhere, the fault does not lie with Him. The blame for a dearth of gift rests with us, with our failure to develop our own gifts, and to recognise and foster the gifts of others. May God help us to 'make full proof of [our] ministry' (2 Tim. 4:5). 'Just as each one has received a gift, use it to serve one another as good stewards of the varied grace of God' (1 Pet 4:10, *NET*).

CHAPTER EIGHT

PARTICIPATION IN THE ASSEMBLY

A TTENDING A GATHERING of the assembly at Corinth must have been a bewildering experience. Brother after brother – and perhaps even some of the sisters – leapt to their feet, pouring forth a confused cacophony of incomprehensible sound, as if to outdo the volubility and volume of the speaker that had gone before. Those who gathered may have their emotions stirred and imaginations heightened, but they must surely have left with ringing ears and throbbing heads. And, all too often, when the ringing subsided and the pain cleared, they found that the excitement and emotion had vanished with them, and left them no more encouraged or instructed, no better off than before. Indeed, it was the tragedy of Corinth that the believers came together 'not for the better, but for the worse' (1 Cor. 11:17).

Clearly, the Corinthians urgently needed corrective teaching, and Paul addresses their failure in unequivocal terms. And we have cause to be thankful that God, in His sovereignty, saw to it that that corrective teaching was preserved in the inspired Word of God. Had it not been for the disorder that prevailed at Corinth, we would have very little direction from Scripture about how an assembly gathering should function. However, Paul's guidance for the assembly in Corinth allows us to understand the principles that should order our gatherings.

It is important to note that, for the most part, the Holy Spirit addressed the situation in Corinth by giving principles, rather than precepts. The apostle did lay out some clear precepts – for example, his instruction that tongues should not be spoken if no interpreter was present (1 Cor. 14:28), or that women should 'keep silence in the churches: for it is not permitted unto them to speak' (v. 34) are not mere suggestions, but carry all the binding force of Divine commands.

The Holy Spirit could have added a whole array of rules to govern the participation in assembly gatherings. He could have laid down a detailed liturgy for the gatherings of God's people. That is exactly what God had done in an earlier dispensation. The exhaustive prescriptions for the collective religious life of the nation of Israel stand in contrast to the limited directions given for the assembly. And that contrast is significant of the great shift that has taken place from the dispensation of Law to the age of grace, when we worship 'in spirit and in truth' (Jn 4:24). Spiritual worship is marked by liberty. By giving principles, rather than precepts, the Holy Spirit preserves the liberty of God's people to use their Divinely-given gift, to worship and serve Him.

With liberty comes variety. Variety was a prominent feature of the assembly meetings at Corinth: 'How is it then, brethren? When ye come together, every one of you hath a psalm, hath a doctrine, hath a tongue, hath a revelation, hath an interpretation' (1 Cor. 14:26). There was variety in who took part – participation was not limited to a single man or a clerical elite, but was open to 'every one of you [brethren]'. There was variety too in how they took part – in song, prayer, or speaking. Paul is not condemning the Corinthian believers for their readiness to participate. Indeed, we would do well to emulate their example. Slow starts and long pauses were not features of the assembly gatherings in Corinth. If we came prepared, as they did, we might well dispense with them too.

But liberty also brings responsibility. Every brother could take part; it did not follow that every brother should take part. Those who came prepared to participate had also to be prepared not to participate. Those who took part had to be guided by two vitally important principles, which Paul outlines in 1 Corinthians 14. The first of these summarises the argument that commenced at the end of chapter 12: 'Let all things be done unto edifying' (1 Cor. 14:26).

This is the 'more excellent way' (12:31) that Paul had promised to show to his readers. It is an approach to the exercise of gift that follows after love (1 Cor. 14:1). We often encounter 1 Corinthians 13 as a general statement about love, detached from its setting in Scripture. But in the context of 1 Corinthians the sphere in which this love is demonstrated is the local assembly, and it is demonstrated by the intelligent exercise of spiritual gift. Thus it is the responsibility of every brother who takes audible part in the gatherings of the assembly to ensure that his contribution is motivated by love, and that it is for the edification – or building up – of the other members of the assembly.

This will have profound and practical implications for what I say and how I say it. It will ensure that what I say is scriptural (1 Cor. 13:10). It will ensure that my contributions are not content-free noise, but carefully chosen words, calculated to bring 'edification, and exhortation, and comfort' (14:3). It will ensure that I speak distinctly, uttering 'words easy to be understood' (14:9). It will affect how I preach and how I pray, and my activity will be marked by the same motive that drove the apostle: 'that by my voice I might teach others also' (vv. 13–19).

This truth has negative implications too. If I am following after love, I will not find myself taking part just to be heard. Love 'vaunteth not itself, is not puffed up' (13:4), and if my participation is ruled by love, I will not get to my feet to impress others with the profundity of my thought or the eloquence of my expression, but to help and encourage them. And I will be less inclined to spend time displaying my knowledge of error, and my ability to refute it, when I remember that love 'rejoiceth not in iniquity, but rejoiceth in the truth' (13:6).

Following after love is not easy or automatic. But though it is demanding it is also indispensable, for without it we will be no more than 'sounding brass, or a tinkling cymbal' – perhaps entertaining, possibly annoying, but of no abiding use (13:1).

It is difficult to read the attributes of love in chapter 13 without thinking of the lovely Man Who uniquely personified love, and eloquently exemplified its every feature. He had 'the tongue of the learned, that [He] should know how to speak a word in season to him that is weary' (Isa. 50:4). His words were not ostentatious – He did 'not cry, nor lift up, nor cause His voice to be heard in the street' (Isa. 42:2). His ministry was not destructive – 'A bruised reed shall He not break, and the smoking flax shall He not quench: He shall bring forth judgment unto truth' (v. 3). 'Never man spake like this man' (Jn 7:46) for 'grace is poured into [His] lips' (Ps. 45:2). How can we not desire to emulate so great an example, to long to speak as He spoke, because we love as He loved?

Later in 1 Corinthians 14, Paul gives a second principle: 'Let all things be done decently and in order' (v. 40). Again, it is important to note that, though this is an excellent maxim for many areas of life, its primary application is to the gatherings of the assembly. This is not a universally popular concept. For many believers, sincerity is identified with spontaneity, and the idea of order seems mere legalistic formality. However, fervour and sincerity do not imply disorder. Indeed, disorder in worship is a denial of the character of a God Who 'is not the author of confusion, but of peace' (v. 33). The exercise of spiritual gift does not destroy self-control, or render it redundant: 'the spirits of the prophets are subject to the prophets' (v. 32). And that self-control is guided by care for the good of others (v. 31) and consideration for the gift of others (v. 30). Spiritual intelligence will, at times, prevent a brother from taking part (vv. 28, 30), and Scriptural obedience will, at all times, ensure that sisters do not take part audibly.

This principle is beautifully exemplified in the conduct of Christ. We see it in the decorum of the Boy Who sat in the Temple hearing the doctors, 'and asking them questions' (Lk.

2:46,47); in the dignity of the Man Who took the scroll and read and expounded the Scriptures in Nazareth (Lk. 4:16–21); and in the indignation of the Son, Whose Father's House had been made a 'den of thieves' (Mk 11:15–17). He did everything 'decently and order', and our behaviour should take its character from Him.

Human beings are creatures of extremes. For many, the worship of God demands a liturgy and clergy – a book that tells us what to say, and a man to say it for us. Others believe that genuine worship is only offered in ecstatic utterances and untrammelled excitement. Either extreme falls far short of the scriptural pattern, where liberty and variety of public participation are preserved and protected by our obedience to the principles of God's Word, and where we can manifest the character of Christ by doing all things unto edification, decently, and in order.

CHAPTER NINE

THE ASSEMBLY AND REWARD

'IT'S NOT ABOUT WINNING, it's about taking part.' These words featured prominently on the walls of the sports hall in my school, intended, presumably, to nerve the faint endeavours of those whose limited sporting skill meant that winning wasn't really an option. But while the slogan might have been helpful in persuading un-athletic teenagers to give their best, it carries little conviction for most sportsmen and women. Their commitment, their sacrifice, and their constant and exhausting efforts are not motivated by mere participation, but by the struggle to improve, to excel, and, above all, to win.

Sadly, though, when it comes to our Christian experience, the platitude often applies far too well – we are happy to settle for just taking part. We are glad to be saved, but we are unmoved by any imperative to attempt or achieve great things for God. We lose sight of the truth that the Christian life is a contest, not in the sense that we are in competition with our fellow-believers, but because we strive to win an imperishable and an eternal crown (1 Cor. 9:25). And if the pursuit of a fading crown commands such dedication from those who pursue them, then the prospect of an eternal and heavenly reward should surely compel us to 'press toward the mark for the prize of the high calling of God in Christ Jesus' (Phil. 3:14).

There are several passages in the New Testament that deal with the review and reward of the believer's service, but 1 Corinthians 3–4 provides one of the most sustained discussions. In 1 Corinthians 3, Paul uses two metaphors to describe the local assembly: 'ye are God's husbandry [tilled field], ye are God's building' (v. 9). Both of these pictures stress that the assembly is a place for hard work – neither a farm nor a building site is a place for idlers. But they also indicate that this work must be orderly – haphazard and uncoordinated activity in either setting would be at best unproductive, and at worst dangerous. And Paul develops the figure of building to teach us that what we build on matters:

> According to the grace of God which is given unto me, as a wise masterbuilder, I have laid the foundation, and another buildeth thereon. But let every man take heed how he buildeth thereupon. For other foundation can no man lay than that is laid, which is Jesus Christ (vv. 10,11).

Paul, by his teaching, laid the foundation of the assembly in Corinth – and of every other New Testament assembly. That foundation must be the basis for our service for God. Paul goes even further than this: 'If any man's work abide which he hath built thereupon, he shall receive a reward' (v. 14). God rewards service that contributes to the upbuilding of the local assembly.

Paul does not conceive of any Christian service that is not based in, or for the benefit – or the establishment – of a local assembly. That is a startling fact, and should cause us each to think carefully about the sphere in which we seek to serve God. It is not for us to evaluate another believer's service, or to say whether it will or will not be rewarded. In the light of this passage, however, it is a grave risk for us to expend our limited resources and our fleeting moments of opportunity by investing them in any service or in any sphere that does not have the mandate of God's Word. After all, as Paul elsewhere points out, using a different picture, 'if anyone competes as an athlete, he will not be crowned as the winner unless he competes according to the rules' (2 Tim. 2:5, NET). How tragic it would be to arrive at the judgement seat of Christ, only to find that our most strenuous and sincere efforts have earned us no reward because we did not take care that we were building on the correct foundation; because we did not 'strive lawfully'.

What we build on is crucial, but so is what we build in. Paul lists six types of material: 'gold, silver, precious stones, wood, hay, stubble' (1 Cor. 3:12). This list divides into two clear categories. The first comprises gold, silver, and precious stones – materials that are valuable and durable. The materials in the second group – wood, hay, and stubble – are bulky but they have little value, and, when subjected to the proving flames of Divine testing, will leave nothing behind. In the light of the judgement seat of Christ, the quality of my service matters far more than the mere quantity.

The apostle's teaching raises some sobering questions for each of us. Does my activity in the assembly build in wood, hay, and stubble – materials that lie near at hand, and that can be gathered without too much effort, inconvenience, or difficulty? Or am I prepared to work hard and dig deep, to expend time and exert effort in order to produce something – however small – that will make a valuable and enduring contribution to the church of God? These questions need to exercise our minds now. It will be too late when we stand at the judgement seat of Christ, and see the efforts that we thought so substantial and praiseworthy reduced to worthless ash, and ourselves standing with empty hands, 'saved, yet so as by fire' (1 Cor. 3:15). And, by contrast, how blessed it will be, when the smoke clears, if there remains something of real value, appreciated and acknowledged by the One Whose 'well done' will mean so incalculably much.

And the passage makes it clear that it is Christ's assessment of our service that matters. Paul states this principle in relation to his own experience:

> But with me it is a very small thing that I should be judged of you, or of man's judgment: yea, I judge not mine own self. For I know nothing by myself; yet am I not hereby justified: but He that judgeth me is the Lord' (1 Cor. 4:3,4).

The phrase 'man's judgment' is more literally translated 'man's day', and, by using it, Paul draws a contrast between a judgement that matters, and one that does not. In man's day, it is man who assesses and evaluates, who measures and acknowledges worth. Such judgement and such reward are of little account in the apostle's eyes. He served with his eye firmly fixed on the day of Christ, when 'the Lord come[s], Who both will bring to light the hidden things of darkness, and will make manifest the counsels of the hearts' (v. 5). These verses do not give licence for a maverick spirit of independence that rides roughshod over the concerns and advice of spiritual believers. But it does mean that my service in the assembly should not be motivated by a desire to please or impress men.

And it is evident from these verses that, in the Divine assessment of our service, motive matters. It is not enough to do the right thing in the right way in the right place. We must serve with the correct motive. And, in chapter 13 of the epistle, Paul identifies the crucial motive, whose absence robs the most redoubtable undertakings of their eternal worth and their capacity to please God. Whatever else I have, or am, or do, if I have not love I am profited nothing, 'I am nothing' (13:2,3). The motive of my service matters more than how impressive or successful it seems. The ultimate accolade of the Master will be 'Well done, thou good and faithful servant' (Mt. 25:21). Not 'popular', not 'esteemed', not 'successful', but 'good' and 'faithful' are the epithets that express Heaven's highest approbation.

It is a wonderful privilege to be a participant in the Christian race. It is marvellous, matchless, and amazing grace that lets us in. But we should not be content to ramble along in the pack, for the grace that lets us in is the grace that lets us win. Any resource or ability that we have was given by God, and yet He will reward us for faithfully using those resources and those abilities in His service. May God help us to live as the apostle did – in the constant anticipation of 'that day' – and let us build our best and highest efforts into the assembly, knowing that our 'labour is not in vain in the Lord' (1 Cor. 15:58).

CHAPTER TEN

RULE IN THE ASSEMBLY

THERE IS SOMETHING uniquely poignant about the events recorded for us in Acts 20. Summoned by the apostle Paul, the elders of the church at Ephesus had made the sixty-mile journey to meet, for one last time, with the apostle whom they loved so dearly, and to whom they owed so much. There, on the shores of the Mediterranean, they wept, embraced, said their final farewells, and received their final message from the apostle.

There was nothing sentimental about Paul's words to them. Faithful in all his ministry, he now seized the opportunity to deliver a stark, clear-eyed warning about the difficulties that lay ahead for the Ephesian church, and for the elders who were responsible for its care:

> Take heed therefore unto yourselves, and to all the flock, over the which the Holy Ghost hath made you overseers, to feed the church of God, which He hath purchased with His own blood. For I know this, that after my departing shall grievous wolves enter in among you, not sparing the flock. Also of your own selves shall men arise, speaking perverse things, to draw away disciples after them. Therefore watch, and remember, that by the space of three years I ceased not to warn every one night and day with tears. And now, brethren, I commend you

to God, and to the word of His grace, which is able to
build you up, and to give you an inheritance among all
them which are sanctified (Acts 20:28–32).

Though the apostle sounded solemn notes of warning, there was
no hint of defeatism in his words. He was leaving the Ephesians
and, in just a short time, the world, but while the Ephesians would
keenly feel his loss, they would not, ultimately, be impoverished
by it, for Paul could, with confidence, commend them to 'God
and the Word of His grace'.

The atmosphere and concerns of Paul's farewell are echoed
and extended in the Pastoral Epistles. Paul's final letters, to
Timothy and Titus, resonate with his awareness that his
ministry is drawing to an end, and that the torch of testimony
is about to be passed to a new generation. They are filled, too,
with his concern for the preservation and communication of
Divine truth – the whole counsel of God.* And repeatedly
they sound the alarm, warning that the precious deposit of
truth is already being assailed, and will come under escalating
attack in the 'perilous times' that mark 'last days' (2 Tim. 3:1).

But bleak though the outlook of the epistles may seem, at
times, to be, it never becomes hopeless. Hope can never give
way to despair, because God has planned and provided an
entity to preserve and proclaim the truth of His Word. That
entity stands in contrast to anything that man has devised. In
contrast with the networks of educational institutions, or
even the power of the military panoply with which men have
often attempted to defend truth against error, it is a simple
entity and – to the human eye at least – a very feeble one. It is
so simple that it needs no complex administrative hierarchy
or impressive physical home. So simple that it can be
composed of no more than two or three believers. So simple,
and yet it is God's essential and irreplaceable means for the
defence and proclamation of His truth in this dispensation.

---

* It is an indication of just how strong this emphasis is that some twelve expressions
that describe Divine revelation occur a total of approximately sixty-nine times in
the three epistles.

Thus it is that the Pastoral Epistles are filled with assembly truth. And because assemblies are made up of individuals and households, and because the way in which I live my life from moment to moment and day to day will have an important impact on the assembly's ability to perform its God-given function, the Pastorals are also full of instruction for individual believers – old and young, male and female, employers and employees. Whether masters or slaves, husbands or wives, parents or children, all have a vital role to play in teaching, defending, adorning, and living 'the truth that is in keeping with godliness' (Tit. 1:1, *NET*).

But these epistles have a special and specific focus on one group of individuals, who have the heaviest responsibility for ensuring that the assembly functions effectively as 'the pillar and ground of the truth' (1 Tim. 3:15). These men are described as elders, for they are mature believers, not novices (1 Tim. 3:6; 5:19; 1 Pet. 5:1). They are described as overseers (Acts 20:28; the KJV, in keeping with its use of existing ecclesiastical titles, translates the same word as 'bishops' in Phil. 1:1; 1 Tim. 3:2; and Tit. 1:7), for it is their responsibility to keep a faithful watch over the flock, to identify and address needs within, and danger without, the assembly. And they are described as shepherds, for theirs is a ministry of care, nourishment, and encouragement, which takes its pattern from ministry of the Chief Shepherd, under Whom they serve (1 Pet. 5:4).

Perhaps nowhere is this point so clearly made as in the first chapter of Titus. Paul opens the chapter by reminding us, as he does so often in the Pastorals, of the glorious truth that God has spoken. And he also emphasises that his apostleship is bound up with this process of revelation.

First, he stresses that his apostleship is 'according to the faith of God's elect' and the 'knowledge of the truth that is in keeping with godliness' (Tit. 1:1, *NET*). Whether 'the faith' in this verse is to be understood as objective (referring to the sum of Divinely revealed truth) or subjective (referring to the confidence that believers place in God) is a contested point. However, given the emphasis on revelation throughout the

opening of this chapter, it seems more likely that it is the body
of truth that is being referred to here.* Thus, Paul is stressing
that his discipleship is firmly based on the Faith that is held
by God's elect and is in accordance with the 'full knowledge'
of the truth, not a defective or distorted version of it. Paul's
ministry is not that of a maverick – his teaching and his life
alike align with the Divine revelation that has been received
and acknowledged by the believers at Crete.

This context also explains Paul's unique description of
himself as 'a servant of God'. This is a title used of Moses   (1
Chron. 6:49; 2 Chron. 24:9; Neh. 10:29; Dan. 9:11) in
connection with the revelation of the Law. So Paul is
positioning himself both as being in full accord with the
revealed truth of God, and as being a channel through which
that truth was communicated. Thus, he has a unique role in
the unfolding of that revelation, in accordance with the
wisdom of the Divine plan:

> In hope of eternal life, which God, that cannot lie,
> promised before the world began; but hath in due times
> manifested His word through preaching, which is
> committed unto me according to the commandment of
> God our Saviour (Tit. 1:2,3).

Paul then seems to move away from this theme, as he gets
down to the business of giving Titus his marching orders – he
is to 'set in order the things that are wanting, and ordain
elders in every city' (v. 5). And, taking up the second element
of this two-part mission first, he outlines the qualities that
must mark an elder – personally, in his home life, and in his
movements before the world. The requirements are rigorous,
and called for men who stood in total contrast to the standards

---

* The alternative view – that 'the faith' here refers to the faith that God's elect have
reposed in God – also creates some difficulties in understanding 'according to'. For
a discussion of this issue, which arrives at a different conclusion to that presented
here, see I. Howard Marshall, *A Critical and Exegetical Commentary on the Pastoral
Epistles*, International Critical Commentary Series (Edinburgh: T&T Clark, 2004),
119–120, and for a robust account of the view that *kata* must be translated as
'according to' see William Kelly, *An Exposition of the Epistle of Paul to Titus*.

and mores of Cretian society, for the elder was not to be a belly
(vv. 6,7), a beast (v. 8), or a liar (v. 9, *cf.* v. 12).

And then, just as we might have begun to wonder why it
was that the requirements of being an elder are so exacting
and specific, Paul gives us the reason, and reveals that he has
never really stopped talking about 'the faith' and 'the truth'
at all. The 'for' that opens verse 10 introduces an explanation,
not just of the requirements of verse 9, but of those outlined
in verses 6, 7, and 8, and the importance of Titus' mission, as
stated in verse 5.* It is because 'there are many unruly and vain
talkers and deceivers' that elders are so important, and
because the mouths of these false teachers will only be
stopped by those whose life and teaching alike carry weight
and conviction, that the standards required are so clearly
delineated.

Titus's mission to Crete had a vital and urgent importance
for, in appointing elders (the ecclesiastical overtones of the
KJV's 'ordain' are misleading), he was putting in place an
essential infrastructure to allow Christian testimony to
continue untainted in Crete, unadulterated alike by the
religious confusion of Cretian society and the enticing lure
of Judaising teaching. Titus carried out this mission as a
delegate of the apostle Paul – this verse gives him his mandate
for a task that was unusual enough to require explicit
instruction. Indeed, the word translated as 'ordain' or
'appoint' (*kathistēmi*) is used of elders in only this passage – it
is used in one other place in relation to the functioning of a
local assembly when, in Acts 6, the apostles instructed the
believers to 'look ... out among you seven men of honest
report, full of the Holy Ghost and wisdom, whom we may
appoint over this business'. On one other occasion we read of
the appointment of elders, when, in Acts 14:23, Paul and
Barnabas 'appointed elders for them in the various churches'
(NET). It is worth noting that 'appointed' here translates a

---

* In each chapter of Titus, 'for' provides a vital hinge between sections that outline
Divine requirements for Christian living and the reasons and resources that make
such living both possible and imperative. See 2:11 and 3:3.

different Greek word (*cheirotoneō*). This word carries the idea of selection, and its only other occurrence in the New Testament is instructive. In 2 Corinthians 8:18,19, Paul speaks of the unnamed brother 'whose praise [was] in the gospel' and 'who was also chosen (*cheirotoneō*) of the churches'. Here the word carries a clear implication of the recognition and selection of one who was qualified, a sense which is equally relevant in relation to the apostolic identification of elders in Acts 14.

Such identification by the apostles or their delegates was the exception, rather than the rule, and when it did happen there was no thought of the conferral or transmission of any sort of sacramental power – the emphasis is, rather, on the public recognition of personal qualification. And that personal qualification would include those characteristics that are outlined with such clarity in Titus 1 and 1 Timothy 3. But while those qualifications were necessary for an elder, they were not in themselves sufficient to make a man an elder. That something additional was required is clear from Paul's words to the Ephesian elders: 'Take heed therefore unto yourselves, and to all the flock, over the which the Holy Ghost hath made you overseers' (Acts 20:28). Whether these elders had been identified by apostolic authority is beside the point – their eldership came not from man, but from God.

Elders, then, are Divinely appointed and equipped for the work that is theirs. But the work of the Holy Spirit requires exercise – and, indeed, ambition – on the part of the individual: 'Here is a trustworthy saying: Whoever aspires to be an overseer desires a noble task' (1 Tim. 3:1, NIV). But, as Peter makes clear, the aspiration must be a spiritual aspiration, and the motives behind it must be pure:

> Feed the flock of God which is among you, taking the oversight thereof, not by constraint, but willingly; not for filthy lucre, but of a ready mind; Neither as being lords over God's heritage, but being ensamples to the flock. And when the chief Shepherd shall appear, ye

shall receive a crown of glory that fadeth not away (1
Pet. 5:2–4).

Peter's language in this passage beautifully expresses another
aspect of the elder's work. The elder must be 'apt to teach' (1
Tim. 3:2) – both able and willing to communicate Divine truth
–the expression demands skill in teaching, and not just
willingness to teach. He must also be able to oppose error – to
handle the Word of God with such clarity and conviction as
to stop the mouths of the teachers of error, whatever their
angle of attack. But he must also be a shepherd, feeding the
flock of God, and leading it by example. And the nature of
that shepherd ministry, with its care and its consideration
and its cost, has been modelled with total perfection by the
Chief Shepherd, under Whom they serve, and for Whose
coming, commendation, and crown they wait. As Peter wrote
these words, his mind must have gone back to the shores of
Galilee, when the risen Christ had given him a threefold
commission: 'feed My lambs ... shepherd My sheep ... feed My
sheep' (Jn 21:15–17, NET). Now, the aged apostle, himself an
elder, takes up the same language as he exhorts his fellow
shepherds to 'feed the flock of God'.

This aspect of the shepherd's work is stressed, too, in 1
Timothy 3:5: 'For if a man know not how to rule his own
house, how shall he take care of the church of God?' The
alteration of the expected parallel here is striking. The elder
must know how to rule his own house, but he must 'take care'
of the church of God. We should not overstate the
significance of the change – the word for rule is used of the
elder in 1 Thessalonians 5:12, 1 Timothy 5:17 and Hebrews 13:17,
24 – but even allowing for this, the difference in emphasis is
striking. And it is very precious to notice the two other
occasions when the word translated 'take care' appears in
Scripture. It is used in Luke 10:34 of the 'good Samaritan' who
went to the bruised and battered man who lay dying by the
side of the road and 'bound up his wounds, pouring in oil and
wine, and set him on his own beast, and brought him to an

inn, and took care of him'. And it is used in the following
verse in the instructions of the Samaritan to the innkeeper:
'Take care of him; and whatsoever thou spendest more, when
I come again, I will repay thee'. There is a lovely picture here
of the ministry of the elder. Like the innkeeper, he has been
commissioned by his absent Lord. Destitute sinners, rescued
from destruction by the Saviour, but still bearing the wounds
and bruises of sin, have been entrusted to his care in the
Saviour's absence. And like the innkeeper, he can be
confident of full recompense for all his efforts when the Chief
Shepherd appears to rapture and reward His own.

Scripture, then, is clear about the responsibilities of the
elder – to teach the truth, to resist error, and to take care of
the flock of God. But the reciprocal responsibilities of that
flock are made equally clear. Believers in assembly fellowship
are to know and esteem their elders, according to 1
Thessalonians 5:12,13:

> And we beseech you, brethren, to know them which
> labour among you, and are over you in the Lord, and
> admonish you; And to esteem them very highly in love
> for their work's sake.

The verb 'to know' here carries with it the idea of perceiving,
of knowing by seeing. Elders are known by their labour (v. 12)
and by their work (v. 13). So Paul is not speaking here of the
recognition of or assent to an ecclesiastical ordination.
Rather, he is calling for the saints – indeed, beseeching them,
which tells us something of the importance of this issue – to
look around, to perceive who it was that was labouring
amongst them and for them, and to recognise that these were
those who were 'over [them] in the Lord'. And, as they
recognised the character of these men, and the taxing and
tiring labour that they undertook, they were to esteem them,
to think highly of them, to give them a special place.

A similar responsibility is outlined in 1 Timothy 5:

> Let the elders that rule well be counted worthy of double
> honour, especially they who labour in the word and

doctrine. For the scripture saith, Thou shalt not muzzle the ox that treadeth out the corn. And, The labourer is worthy of his reward (1 Tim. 5:17,18).

Notice again the emphasis on the elder's exertions – the word 'labour' means 'to labour with wearisome effort, to toil'.* And, in this Pastoral Epistle, as in Titus, there is an emphasis on the sphere of that labour, and the elder's responsibility in the defence and communication of truth. And there are two aspects to that labour – labouring in the Word to learn its truth, and in teaching to communicate it. And men who make this effort, who engage in the exhaustive and exhausting study of God's Word and who teach it to the saints, are to 'be counted worthy of double honour', respected in a special way by the saints among whom they serve. And that honour may be very practically expressed – the quotations from Deuteronomy 25:4 and Luke 10:7 in verse 18 embrace the idea of financial support, though they are not limited to it. Once again, the scriptural ideal for rule in the assembly is clear – exercised elders, equipped by the Holy Spirit and energetically engaged in ruling and teaching, are recognised and appreciated by the flock for which they care. Men like this do not need to demand double honour, for their lives and work command it.

Believers are also responsible to obey elders. The writer to the Hebrews draws his epistle to a close with the exhortation:

> Obey them that have the rule over you, and submit yourselves: for they watch for your souls, as they that must give account, that they may do it with joy, and not with grief: for that is unprofitable for you (Heb. 13:17).

It is striking that this verse is, at once, the clearest statement of the believer's responsibility to the overseers in the assembly and the clearest and most solemn of the overseers' responsibility to their Lord. And if we understand the latter

* Joseph H. Thayer, *Thayer's Greek-English Lexicon of the New Testament* (Peabody, MA: Hendrickson Publishers, 1995), *sv.*

responsibility, if we appreciate that the overseers who rule in God's assembly are neither petty despots not mere administrators, but shepherds who are directly responsible to the Chief Shepherd, and who will answer to Him for their care of our souls, then obedience and submission will seem the obvious response, lest we add to the burden that they carry, and cause tears where there should be joy. It is easy to murmur, to carp and criticise and complain. But before we do so, we should remember the solemn lesson that Moses taught the children of Israel who murmured against his leadership:

> The LORD heareth your murmurings which ye murmur against him: and what are we? Your murmurings are not against us, but against the LORD (Exod. 16:8).

Rebellion against Divinely appointed leadership is rebellion against God. The Israelites thought that they were complaining about God's servant, but the reality was far more serious – they were lifting their voice in complaint against God. Such was the case, too, in the days of Samuel. As the heartbroken judge prayed about the nation's demand for a king, God's response highlighted something much worse than the wounded heart of the nation's devoted servant: 'they have not rejected thee, but they have rejected Me, that I should not reign over them' (1 Sam. 8:7). If we rightly understood the position that elders occupy, and the weight of the burden that comes with that position, it would silence many of our petulant protests and quell so much of our discontent.

Too often, elders have their burden augmented by the murmurings and criticisms of the saints. Their position as leaders also makes them particularly vulnerable to attack by those who level false accusations against them. The Scriptures take account of this, specifying the standard of proof that must be reached before an accusation against an elder can be received:

Against an elder receive not an accusation, but before
two or three witnesses. Them that sin rebuke before all,
that others also may fear (1 Tim. 5:19,20).

The requirement for multiple witnesses to the truth of an
allegation helps to protect elders against malicious
accusations from disgruntled believers who seek to settle
scores and vent their feelings by falsely charging those in
authority. And those who are guilty of sinning in this way are
to be publicly rebuked, so that the other believers in the
assembly are left in no doubt about the seriousness of
undermining Divinely appointed leaders by attempted
character assassination.

Thus, the Word of God clearly and solemnly teaches the
responsibilities of the shepherds and the flock. The
shepherds are to feed, to tend, and to teach. They are vigilant
for attack from without, and for need within. Their burden is
heavy, for they must give account for the souls for whom they
care. But their reward is great, for there is for them 'a crown
of glory which fadeth not away'. The flock is responsible to
know its shepherds, to perceive the diligent exercise of
Divine enablement. They are to esteem, to honour, and to
obey those whom God has raised to lead.

Scripture sets a high standard for rule in God's assembly.
Too often, human failure on the part of shepherds or of the
flock has led to the introduction of human expedients that
have no place in the Word of God, or in His assembly. A one-
man ministry, elected elders (or a distinction between a
teaching elder and other elders), or central rule by bishop,
presbytery, or metropolitan committee are all alike
departures from the Divine pattern, no matter how well
intentioned or, from a human perspective, seemingly sensible
they are. God's way is both far more simple and far more
difficult. It is simple because it eschews human machinery
and relies on the work of the Holy Spirit to equip and exercise
men to do the work of an overseer, to 'labour in the word and
in doctrine', to stop the mouths of false teachers, and to watch

for the souls of the saints. But it is difficult, for it calls for men of sterling character, who are not marked by the vices of the age, and who are willing, with God's help, to labour to the point of exhaustion to 'take care of the flock of God'. May God help us to honour and esteem leaders of this calibre and quality.

CHAPTER ELEVEN

THE LORD AND THE LAMPSTANDS (1)

ONE OF THE FIRST THINGS we do when we begin to study a book of the Bible is to outline the structure of the book and the skeleton of its argument. Of course, all books are not equally easy to outline. When we get to Revelation, however, we have the easiest task of all, for the book comes with its own outline: 'Write the things which thou hast seen, and the things which are, and the things which shall be hereafter' (1:19).

'The things which shall be hereafter' comprises the largest section of the book, from chapter 4 to 22. It is worth noting in passing that this verse clearly confirms the futurist reading of Revelation 4–22 – the chapters describe future events, not first-century history (as suggested by preterism) or principles relevant throughout the Church age (idealism). 'The things which are' describes chapters 2 and 3 – the letters to the seven churches. Respected Bible teachers have seen in these letters a historical-prophetical overview of the dispensation of grace, but it is important to remember that Christ addresses seven local churches that actually existed at that time. It is also vital to grasp that the strengths and weaknesses that these individual assemblies display have marked Christian testimony throughout the centuries. We cannot park the failure of these churches safely in the past; Christ's words are still relevant to us. 'The things which thou hast seen' describes the vision of chapter 1. John's description of that vision is not merely a preface to the book – it is an essential part of 'the revelation of Jesus Christ'. An adequate consideration of this vision would fill a volume; here we can only notice briefly some important points.

First, we should notice the *designation* of Christ in the vision. He is introduced as 'Alpha and Omega, the first and the last' (v. 11). Both of these titles emphasise the comprehensiveness of Christ. As the 'Alpha and Omega', He is not only the complete revelation of God, but He is also the One 'in Whom are hid all the treasures of wisdom and knowledge' (Col. 2:3). And the practical implications of this tremendous truth become beautifully clear as we read through the letters to the churches. Every one of these assemblies was based in a different context, and each faced individual and distinctive challenges. They are addressed in different ways. Not all are praised, not all are rebuked. But each church's letter begins with a fresh revelation of Christ, specially designed to address their individual needs. No matter what the difficulties or departure, Christ was sufficient. He alone was – and is – the answer to the needs of each assembly. 'The First and the Last' is a title that appears three times in Revelation, and three times in the prophecy of Isaiah. In both books, it is addressed to God's people at a time when their world has been turned upside down by the rise and fall of earthly empires. How precious to these believers, who must have felt themselves to be little more than flotsam on the breakers of time, was the reminder that they lived their lives under the watchful eye of One Who stands outside of time, the First and the Last.

Then we should notice the *description* of the Lord. First, John sees 'One like unto the Son of man' (v. 13). This is a highly significant and resonant title. It is more than just a reference to the humanity of the Lord Jesus. Rather, the title evokes Daniel's vision of the 'One like the Son of man', Who was brought near before the Ancient of Days, and to Whom:

> there was given ... dominion, and glory, and a kingdom, that all people, nations, and languages, should serve Him: His dominion is an everlasting dominion, which

shall not pass away, and His kingdom that which shall not be destroyed' (Dan. 7:13,14).

It is a title that speaks of Christ's authority to rule over earth, and relates particularly to His Millennial reign. As such, it seems a little out of place in a passage that deals with testimony in the Church age, but it is no accident that it is used here. Instead, this description reminds us of the profound truth that, in the dispensation of grace, the assembly is the place where heavenly administration is seen on earth. In Genesis 28:17, Jacob arose from his dream to acknowledge that 'this is none other but the house of God; this is the gate of heaven'. The place of Divine residence was also the place of Divine administration. And, as the Saviour introduced His disciples to the idea of the local church, He, likewise, associated the two concepts. The promise of His presence 'where two or three are gathered' is linked to a promise that, in the assembly, the administration of Heaven would be manifest on earth: 'whatsoever ye shall bind on earth shall be bound in heaven: and whatsoever ye shall loose on earth shall be loosed in heaven' (Mt. 18:18). The presence of the 'One like unto the Son of man' in the midst of the lampstands reminds us of the unique position occupied by the assembly in this age. It is not merely a gathering of like-minded Christians, but it is God's golden lampstand, in truth, 'an awesome place, ... the house of God... the gate of heaven' (Gen. 28:17, NET)!

In this description, Christ is presented as a priest – His 'garment down to the foot' is priestly attire, and He stands amidst the lampstands, just as the Old Testament priest ministered before the seven-branched lampstand in the Holy Place. And just as the Aaronic priest tended the lamp, to ensure that its light shone brightly, so, in His censure and His praise, the great High Priest makes the adjustments required to ensure that the light of testimony shines brightly in a night-time scene.

Every element of this description is calculated to reveal the character of Christ. His holiness and majesty are evident in the golden girdle, which speaks of affections controlled by Divine righteousness, in the whiteness of His hairs and head, demonstrating His purity and maturity, in the fine bronze of His feet and in His voice, as sublimely powerful as the roaring of great cataracts. He is the one Who sees all – the blowtorch intensity of the blazing flame of His eyes has the power to pierce and penetrate any pretence or hypocrisy. And what He sees, He can correct, for 'out of His mouth went a sharp two edged sword' (v. 16). The chapters that follow bear ample witness to the intensity of His scrutiny – repeatedly He says 'I know'. And they bear testimony too to the surgical precision of the two edged sword – identifying and excising error, cutting and cleansing, but so carefully wielded as to inflict no unnecessary injury, cause no collateral damage.

And He has the right to chasten, for He holds the seven stars in His right hand. These 'seven stars are the angels of the seven churches' (v. 20). The lampstands present the assemblies as seen on earth, the stars present a heavenly perspective. The position of these in the Saviour's hand demonstrates His ownership – they are His. But they are in His right hand, not just a possession, but something prized and protected, shielded with Divine power. These churches were battered by many assaults, from physical persecution to the seduction of false teaching. But they did not weather these storms alone. However daunting the onslaught, they were held fast in the right hand of the Alpha and Omega, the First and the Last.

So intense is His holiness, and so overwhelming His majesty, that even John, who had leaned on His breast, 'fell at His feet as dead' (v. 17). This is the One Who moves in the midst of the lampstands, and Who has promised His presence in our midst as we gather. We love to claim that promise, but we often do so with a lightness that suggests that we have not sufficiently contemplated the revelation of Christ in this chapter. If we really caught the radiance of His holiness, if we really felt the intensity of His gaze, we would understand that it is not a light thing to gather where He is in the midst. May God grant that all that is careless and casual will melt away in the glare of His transcendent glory, and that the golden lampstands will stand firm and shine 'forth the praises of Him who hath called [us] out of darkness into His marvellous light (1 Pet. 2:9).

CHAPTER TWELVE

THE LORD AND THE LAMPSTANDS (2)

R EVELATION 1 PRESENTS US with a unique view of the
Lord Jesus Christ. In transcendent glory He stands in the
midst of seven golden lampstands, tending them with priestly
care. His position and His splendour alike ensure that He is
the cynosure of the scene, the focal point to which our gaze is
drawn. That is John's purpose. His book is 'the revelation of
Jesus Christ' not just in the sense that it communicates a
revelation belonging to, and given by, the Lord, but because
it reveals Christ.

In the previous chapter, we have considered something of
this revelation. Now we want to think a little about the other
remarkable feature of John's vision. Having contemplated the
Lord, we want now to learn something about the lampstands.

Notice first the situation of these lampstands.
Geographically, the assemblies that they represent were
arranged in a horseshoe shape in present-day Turkey. Some
have speculated that the lampstands followed the same
arrangement. However, the crucial point is not how the
lampstands are placed in relation to each other, but how they
are positioned in relation to the Lord. And that position is
conveyed most clearly in the passage – and repeated for
emphasis. Christ is 'in the midst' of the lampstands (1:13; 2:1).
His position is one of centrality, emphasising the uniqueness
of His relationship to these companies where He dwells, and
which He has 'purchased with His own blood' (Acts 20:28).
No one else could rightfully take that central place – it is His,

and His alone. His position also demonstrates His care for these assemblies. He is not remote or distant. He moves amongst them in priestly ministry, with an intimate closeness and care. And that care was equally available to each of these assemblies. Their condition varied, yet no assembly could claim a monopoly on or even a majority of Christ's interest, or of His ability to address their varied and individual needs.

Another striking feature of these lampstands is their separateness. In the Holy Place of the Tabernacle there was the seven-branched lampstand. Its seven branches were all joined to one base, a fitting representation of a nation that found in Jerusalem a common gathering centre. John's vision differed crucially from this. Each of the seven lampstands that he saw stood upon its own base, without any physical link to any of the other six. Something radically different from the federal nature of Judaism is depicted in these lampstands. It is not altogether easy to find a term that expresses the truth that is presented by the separateness of the lampstands. Quite often it is termed the autonomy of the local assembly. That may be the best term available in English, but it is less than ideal. 'Autonomy' is made up of the Greek words for 'self' and 'law' and literally means 'making a law for oneself'. That, of course, should not be an accurate description of any assembly. But if the truth is difficult to summarise in a word, it is vividly presented in this vision. The relationship that matters here is not that between individual assemblies. Rather, the focus is on the relationship between each assembly and the One Who stands in the midst of the lampstands. Fellowship between assemblies is important. The New Testament provides numerous examples of the way in which assemblies can help and encourage each other. But it never countenances any idea of grouping assemblies together, of creating structures of federation or hierarchy. Instead, each assembly is directly answerable to Christ. His is the only presiding function – He stands alone amidst the lampstands.

As we consider the appearance of the lampstands, we must also notice their supply. Contrary to what the translators of the KJV suggest, they are not candlesticks. Nor are they lamps. Rather, they are lampstands. That is, they do not themselves produce light. Their function is to hold the oil lamp aloft, in order that its light might be seen. Again, the picture eloquently represents the function of the local assembly. The assembly cannot produce light by itself. It is the 'pillar ... of the truth' (1 Tim. 3:15) radiating the light of Divine truth in a dark and dismal world. It was just such language that the apostle used to describe the assembly in Philippi: 'That ye may be blameless and harmless, the sons of God, without rebuke, in the midst of a crooked and perverse nation, among whom ye shine as lights in the world; holding forth the word of life' (Phil. 2:15,16). No assembly – and no group of assemblies – is the source of truth. We are rightly grateful for all those who help us to understand the truth of God's Word. Nonetheless, we are on dangerous ground if we fail to recognise that what the brethren – with an upper or lower case 'b' – have taught or do teach has no authority if it is not firmly based upon the truth of Scripture. We should notice too that these lampstands bore oil lamps. That surely reminds us of the role of the Holy Spirit. In our collective as well as our individual testimony, we are utterly dependent upon the unending supply of Divine energy if the light is to shine as it should.

Finally, we should not miss the significance of the substance from which these lampstands are fashioned. They are golden lampstands. That immediately speaks of their value. In the biblical economy, gold is the most precious substance found on earth. Related to the value of gold is its beauty. Even the unworked metal is attractive. When worked by the skilled hands of the goldsmith it acquires a beauty that can take the breath away. Throughout history, gold has been the material of choice for the most important, significant, and beautiful objects.

How fitting, then, that it is used to picture that which is of unique and excelling value to Christ. No matter how small the assembly or how humble its members, it has a value to Christ that is not matched by the most glittering and distinguished institutions of earth. It is easy to lose sight of this, to look around on a Lord's Day morning at a handful of saints quavering their uncertain way through a hymn, and to wonder whether it is really worth making the effort to keep going. But if we could see it as Christ does, if we had the spiritual intelligence to catch amidst earthly weakness the gleam of the heavenly gold, we would realise that even the frailest assembly has an immeasurable and incomparable value to Christ, and therefore deserves all of our commitment, energy, and involvement.

But gold, in Scripture, speaks of more than material value and beauty. In its uncorroding incorruptibility it speaks of Deity, of Divine glory, worth, and righteousness. We have already seen it linked with Christ, in the girdle that He wears. The Tabernacle and the Temple alike gleamed with the glory of beaten gold. It was not used in these structures to attract the eye of man, or impress the passing observer – most of the gold was invisible to all but the priests. But the gold was there to manifest the character of God, to reveal His intrinsic glory and His impeccable holiness. And the lampstands are golden for the very same reason – the church of God should take its character from God, and should manifest that character in the world. His greatness, His righteousness, His power should be seen in us. What Paul wished for the assembly in Corinth should be true of any assembly:

> But if all prophesy, and there come in one that believeth not, or one unlearned, he is convinced of all, he is judged of all: and thus are the secrets of his heart made manifest; and so falling down on his face he will worship God, and report that God is in you of a truth' (1 Cor. 14:24,25).

In the two chapters that follow, Christ will address seven local assemblies. As He acknowledges their successes and admonishes them for their failures, He provides instruction that is relevant for all assemblies, everywhere, until He returns. That instruction is always challenging, and frequently humbling. But before that essential and enduring teaching is given, we are caused to see the Lord and the lampstands, reminded that there is One 'Who tends with sweet unwearied care the flock for which He bled' and that companies of His people, though little esteemed by the surrounding world, are of incalculable value and immense importance to His eye, to His mind, and to His heart.

CHAPTER THIRTEEN

LABOUR, LEARNING, AND LOVE IN THE ASSEMBLY

THE CHURCH IS NOT IN THE OLD TESTAMENT. Whether we think of it dispensationally – as the Body of Christ – or locally, there is no revelation of it from Genesis to Malachi. A firm grasp of this fact is a powerful antidote to hermeneutical headaches and doctrinal errors.

There are, however, Old Testament passages that, from our privileged historical perspective, illustrate church truth. In this article, we want to turn our eyes to Bethlehem at the time of the barley harvest and to think of the welcome, the work, and the wealth that a Moabite girl called Ruth found in the field of Boaz. This application is not without scriptural warrant. 1 Corinthians 3:9 describes the assembly as 'God's husbandry' – God's farmland, or cultivated field, and we can learn lessons about the assembly by considering Boaz's field.

The first thing that we learn about this field is that it is a place of *lordship*. Guided by Divine providence, Ruth found her way to a part of the field that was different from any other because it 'belonged to Boaz' (Ruth 2:3). And because it belonged to Boaz, he had authority over it. When he instructed the reapers, their response was not dispute or delay, but obedience. And what was true of Boaz's field is still true of God's husbandry. The assembly is not mine and it is not ours. It belongs to God, and is under the Lordship of Christ. As such, the clear commands of His Word are not to be debated or denied, but demand our absolute and unequivocal obedience. But we should notice that there was nothing grudging or constrained about the obedience of the reapers to Boaz. They obeyed him not because they had to, but because they wanted to. Their respect and affection for their master are evident from the moment that we encounter Boaz. Our obedience to the Word of God should have a similar character. Our love for Christ should produce a willing submission that is as far removed from a costive and rigid legalism as it is from a casual and laissez-faire lack of conviction.

Boaz's field was also marked by *leadership*. The unnamed 'servant that was set over the reapers' provides us with a most precious picture of the Spirit's ministry in a local assembly. Boaz's field was not a place of haphazard activity, where each individual decided whether, and when, and how to work. Each reaper had their allotted duty. The assembly, too, should be marked by orderly activity under the direction and energy of the Holy Spirit. He equips believers for service, providing gifts 'to every [one] severally as He will' (1 Cor. 12:11). And, as He furnishes the gift, He provides the direction and guidance for the exercise of that gift.

The leadership of the servant was essential because the field was a place of *labour*. Ruth and the other reapers were not in the field to picnic – they were there to work. And the work of reaping must have been hard, back-breaking work, under the heat of the Bethlehem sun. But the harvest had to be gathered, and there was no time to stand idle. Ruth epitomised this – it is not hard to hear the respect in the servant's voice as he described her consistent, committed efforts to Boaz: 'she came, and hath continued even from the morning until now, that she tarried a little in the house' (v. 7). God's field, too, is a place for labourers, for hard work and unrelenting effort. All too often, the number of spectators – and commentators – far exceeds the number of those who are prepared to bend their backs to the work of the assembly.

Notice too that Ruth found in Boaz's field a place of *lavish provision*. It is precious to notice Boaz's care that her needs were met. When she was thirsty, she could freely drink of the water that the young men had drawn (v. 9). At mealtime, she was invited to 'come ... hither, and eat of the bread, and dip thy morsel in the vinegar'. And, as if that were not enough, she received a portion from Boaz's own hand, for 'he reached her parched corn, and she did eat, and was sufficed' (v. 14). And even that did not exhaust the provision for after she gathered up the 'handfuls of purpose' (v. 16) left for her by Boaz's instruction, she made her way back home to Naomi with her back bowed by the abundance of what she had gleaned. And this was no once-off bestowal of blessing, but the beginning of many days of bounty, as Ruth gleaned 'unto the end of barley harvest and of wheat harvest' (v. 23).

The assembly should be a place of provision, where the spiritual needs of the child of God are abundantly met. There should be variety in that provision – something of the refreshment of the water, the sustenance of the parched corn, the nourishment of the bread, and the piquancy of the vinegar. We ought to enjoy what is drawn out for us by the effort of others, what has been prepared at home, and presented to us in the assembly. We should go home with a portion to thresh out, to feed our soul to meet the challenges of each day. We should enjoy those blessed moments when the Lord Himself reaches to us just what we need to be sufficed in our need. Sadly, the ideal is not always the reality. But before we conclude that the assembly has failed us, and long before we start to think of looking elsewhere for spiritual food, let us remember that Ruth would have starved had she not been prepared to labour. Her return was proportional to her effort. The more we put into the assembly – the more we attend, the more we pray, the more we prepare – the more we will get out, and the more our souls will be nourished by the baffling bounty of God's Word.

When Ruth returned home with her ephah of barley, Naomi was quick to realise that she had found somewhere exceptional to glean. And as she learned more of the remarkable way in which Divine providence had guided Ruth, she was quick to stress that the field of Boaz was to be a place of *loyalty*: 'It is good, my daughter, that thou go out with his maidens, that they meet thee not in any other field' (v. 22). We still need Naomi's warning. The fields of denominational, interdenominational, and para-church service sometimes look very green. At times, they may offer us opportunities for service that the assembly does not. But we need to learn the lesson that Ruth did – loyalty to Boaz meant loyalty to His field, where his lordship was owned, and his commands obeyed. And if the invitations are hard to decline, the opportunities appealing, and the decisions difficult, let us think what it would mean if not just the other reapers, but our returning Lord found us investing our efforts and our energy in something or some place contrary to the pattern of God's Word.

Above all, perhaps, the field of Boaz was a place of *learning* and of *love*. Before Ruth's story comes to an end, we will find her at Boaz's feet in private communion. We will find her at his side as his bride. And it was in his field that her knowledge of him increased, and her love correspondingly grew. How eagerly she must have set out for the field each morning, knowing that the one she loved would be there. How quickly the day must have passed, for all the exertion it involved. How she must have loved the place where she enjoyed the presence, the provision, and the person of her redeemer.

The New Testament assembly is God's husbandry, God's building. It is the house of God, the pillar and ground of truth. It is Divine in its origin and its character, a light-bearing golden lampstand in a night time scene, the place on earth where, in this dispensation, the administration of Heaven is seen. Nowhere and nothing else can claim this character, these titles, or this status. But nothing could make it more precious than the truth that Christ is present there. May we love it and prize it as He does, and labour there steadfastly until He comes.

www.ingramcontent.com/pod-product-compliance
Lightning Source LLC
Chambersburg PA
CBHW071103090426
42737CB00013B/2446